UNLOCK!

ESCAPE ADVENTURE PUZZLE BOOK

Special thanks to Julien Andre, François Doucet, and Philippe Mouret at Space Cowboys Studio, and to Danielle Robb at Asmodee Entertainment.

Based on the Unlock! system created by Cyril Demaegd. Unlock! Escape Room Adventure Game scenarios designed by Cyril Demaegd (The Formula), Vincent Goyat (Squeek & Sausage), and Guillaume Montiage (Lost in the Timewarp!).

Published in 2021 by Welbeck, an imprint of Welbeck Non-Fiction Limited, part of Welbeck Publishing Group, 20 Mortimer Street, London, W1T 3JW

A CIP catalogue record for this book is available from the British Library

Design: Luke Griffin and Russell Knowles
Editorial: Chris Mitchell

ISBN 978-1-78739-599-2

Printed in Dubai

10 9 8 7 6 5 4 3 2 1

The publishers would like to thank the following sources for their kind permission to reproduce the pictures in this book. All images created by Pierre Santamaria, Legruth, and Cyrille Bertin with the exception of:
Griffixdesign: 19
Shutterstock: Bborriss.67; /Pablo Caridad 10; /Ben Chart: 79, 84, 86, 86, 90, 92, 94, 96, 106, 108, 126, 132, 140, 142; /Business stock 40, 50, 58; /Chempina 168; /doomu 27; /I'm Friday 22, 48, 66 /IlonaBa 17; /Dr. Norbert Lange 57; /Phonlamai Photo 76; /Aleksandr Petrunovskyi 44; /Sashkin 65; /Silmairel 163; /Iurii Stepanov 30; /temp-64GTX 21, 25; /Zentilia 16
Unsplash: /Birmingham Museums Trust 21, 25; /Pawel-Czerwinski 38; /Brett Jordan 62; / Morning Brew 57, 72; /Boris Rabtsevich 70; /Rich Smith 60, 68
Additional textures provided by:
Shutterstock: Art Painter/Ben Chart/Dmitr1ch/KsanaGraphica. Unsplash by Roland Deason & Annie Spratt. Textures.com

Every effort has been made to acknowledge correctly and contact the source and/or copyright holder of each picture and Welbeck Publishing apologises for any unintentional errors or omissions, which will be corrected in future editions of this book.

UNLOCK!

ESCAPE ADVENTURE PUZZLE BOOK

WRITTEN BY JASON WARD

CREATED BY CYRIL DEMAEGD

WELBECK

Contents

Introduction

Welcome to the *Unlock! Escape Adventure Puzzle Book*. Whether you are already familiar with the Unlock! card games, or this is your first Unlock! experience, we hope you enjoy this new way to experience the puzzling adventures ahead of you.

Over the course of this book, you will be given the opportunity to play three different scenarios. These each have very different storylines, but they are united by a unifying concept: you will have to find objects, figure out how to use them, solve puzzles and discover codes in order to progress from room to room (or time period to time period!).

Before you start, it is of *vital importance* that you read the How to Play section on page 6. This book should not be read from cover to cover like a normal book. Instead, you will have to flip around scenarios based on the "page numbers" in the top corners of each page, the numbers that you discover when finding or combining objects, and the codes that you uncover.

Feel free to try to complete the book on your own or, like with physical escape rooms, solve it as part of a group. And, if you are competitive, note down how many penalties you receive along your journey and then challenge another person or group to see if they can do better. Above all, though, have fun!

Good luck.

UNLOCK! Unlocked:
How to Play

Game overview

Based on the popular Unlock! card series, the *Unlock! Escape Adventure Puzzle Book* provides three different adventures: The Formula, Squeek & Sausage and Lost in the TimeWarp!. To complete these missions you will have to solve puzzles, combine objects, figure out codes and make your way through strange, perilous environments, overcoming challenges that will push your creative thinking and deductive skills to their limits.

Navigation

Important: do not look through a scenario before starting to play, or you will spoil the experience for yourself. Read the adventure's introduction and then turn over to the first page. Advancement through each adventure occurs in a non-linear fashion: you shouldn't turn to the next sequential page unless you're specifically told that you can. Instead, the next page you're able to visit is likely to be somewhere else entirely. Each page is numbered or labelled in the top corner and so if you end up with a number – say, 81 – or a letter – say, H – you need to find that page and turn to it in order to continue your adventure. If you'd like to retrace your steps, most pages will outline significant locations that you may return to.

Notebook

Along with the introduction, you'll find a notebook at the start of each adventure. As you'll be leaping back and forth between pages, this is an invaluable resource which allows you to keep track of page numbers, objects and their associated numbers, codes, record your penalties and make other useful notes. For the best playing experience, we strongly recommend that you make good use of of it.

Cards

Alongside the developing story and navigational information, each page includes different "cards".
There are several card types:

- Objects (Red or Blue circle)
- Machines (Green circle)
- Codes (Yellow circle)
- Other cards (Grey circle)

⚫ ⚪ Objects (Red or Blue circle):

Objects can sometimes interact with other objects – for example, a key with a door. To combine two objects, just add their respective numbers (given within a red or blue circle) together, and if their total corresponds to a page number in the adventure, you may turn to that page. A red number can ONLY be combined with a blue number, and vice versa. No other combination is possible – letters cannot be added together, nor other types of cards. Occasionally, an incorrect combination will lead you to a penalty page, so think carefully about why you'd want to combine two objects. Not all combinations lead to a page – penalty or otherwise.

⚫ Machines (Green circle)

There are machines within each adventure that need to be used correctly in order to progress. Each one is unique and needs to be solved in its own way, but the instructions will usually give you some guidance.

⚫ Codes (Yellow circle)

During the game, players will sometimes need to find certain 4- or 5-digit codes in order to unlock items like combination locks and electronic keypads. When you think you've deduced a code, add it to your notebook and turn to the listed page. Once there, you will find out if you were correct: you will have to take a penalty if you've guessed the wrong code, but you may still progress.

⚫ Other cards (Grey circle)

These cards can be:
· A place showing a room and the objects within.
· The result of an interaction with an object.
· A penalty applied to players who made a mistake.

Penalties

The end-game score will be determined by your number of penalties. Penalties are accrued by heading to certain incorrect pages or by incorrectly solving puzzles. The book will always tell you when you're supposed to take a penalty.

Hidden objects

All objects are not always visible. Every now and then, players must look carefully at the "card" images in order to find hidden numbers or letters. Once you discover them, you become able to turn to that page. You will also be able to return to your previous location afterwards.

End of game

The adventure ends once you've managed to solve the last puzzle. The solutions are at the back of the book, starting on p.218.

THE
FORMULA

PENALTIES (X):

ROOM PAGES:

RED NUMBER (OBJECT):

BLUE NUMBER (OBJECT):

CODES:

OTHER NOTES:

MISSION #MK-053	SEP 30 1961	TOP SECRET

1. Objectives

The Department is concerned by the lack of recent reports from Dr Hoffmann. This genius chemist is involved in the MK project.

In his last report, he claimed that his "truth serum" was close to the required reliability. We want Hoffman and his Formula.

2. Means

The team will be taken to the subway station (████████) and will infiltrate the lab, which opens with the code (████████).

You must recover the serum **at any cost**.

You hesitantly make your way through a maze of New York's subway tunnels. It's dark, damp and you feel unnervingly alone. Your briefing was low on details, and you were left dubious about whether this genius Hoffmann was to be trusted or not. A truth serum would certainly make your job easier, but in the wrong hands… you shudder at the thought.

You are trying to be stealthy as you are not quite sure what lies in wait for you, but every little noise that you make echoes loudly before being swallowed by the darkness that stretches both ahead and behind you. Why would your superiors send you – alone! – to investigate, if everyone was on the same team? Something doesn't add up and it makes your skin crawl.

THE FORMULA

After some time you approach your target, just as the briefing described. In the middle of the tracks, you find a trap door in the ground. It's open and light shows through it. Is someone expecting you?

You climb down through the trap door, your hands cold against the metal of the ladder. It's not long before you reach the source of the light, though. Blinking after having spent so much time in the darkness, you step into what appears to be some sort of reception room. While your eyes adjust to the glare of the artificial light you hear a sudden clang from above you.

It appears the hatch through which you entered has been closed. So you weren't alone…

Suddenly, you hear a synthesized voice: "Self-destruction engaged. 60 minutes." Well, that's reassuring. At least your instinct not to trust this mission has not let you down, for whatever good that did you now. There had better be a way out of here!

First, you decide to climb back up to test the hatch door. Locked, as you suspected it would be. No direction to go except forward, it would seem. There is nothing else to do but to explore your surroundings, so you begin to look around the room. You clearly don't have much time, so you try to take in as much as possible at once, and at some speed. Directly across from you is a door. No place better to start than there, you decide.

It's pretty clear that this is the exit. You wrench at the handle, but it's firmly locked, just like the hatch. In any event you must find the Formula first!

The door is almost certainly controlled by this keypad. It's not like any you have seen before, and you have quite some experience with keypads.

For now, you only allow yourself a cursory glance at each object, and you can then return to investigate them all further in more detail, once you have examined the whole room.

A wall-mounted telephone behind a small table. Perhaps you could ring for back up if things get desperate? Unfortunately, there is no dial tone.

A small box with a hole in it. You peer in and you can make out a key attached to a cork. Frustratingly, it's too deep to reach.

Despite the wooden box attached to the wall's flimsy appearance, it seems impervious to your slightly desperate attempts to break it apart by force. If only a sledgehammer were part of the standard espionage toolkit. Next to the seemingly indestructible box is an ancient-looking control panel.

When you click the buttons, nothing happens. It appears to have no electrical supply, and is defunct. Right now, at least, this will be of no use to you.

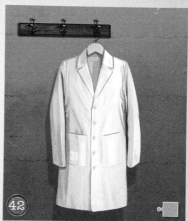

A lab coat hangs on the wall. Judging from the size of it, and the personal details of his height and weight that you had read in his file, it is probably Hoffmann's.

The coat told you two things: the first is that his lab is nearby. And the second is that because it is hanging here, and that he is not wearing it, you are reassured that he is not currently present in the lab. That's one less thing to worry about.

You had almost completed your lap of the room, but you were conscious of the minutes that were slipping by all too quickly. You approach another door, this one apparently to the generator room.

After inspecting it, you realise that you are securely locked into a room that has just announced that it is going to self-destruct in less than an hour. There has to be something else available to you in this room that will help you find a way through one of those doors.

To continue searching the reception room, turn to the pages numbered 10.

The door is locked, of course. Even though you expected it, your palms still begin to sweat as your fears are confirmed.

You walk over to the desk that you had ignored in your initial search. There were a number of objects on it, placed seemingly quite haphazardly. There was nothing that looked out of place in the lab at first glance, but if your training had taught you anything, it was that even the most innocuous object might have great importance, as long as you were willing to look at it in the right way.

The projector looks slightly the worse for wear. Perhaps Dr Hoffmann has an extensive slide collection? No slides to be found here, though.

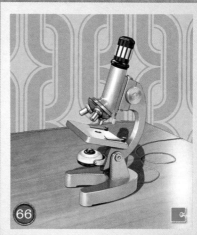

The microscope is very modern. State of the art, even. The lab is clearly very well funded to leave a kit like that lying around.

You have now examined everything of interest in the room. It is clear that you need to get through one of the doors. The other option of remaining in a room set to self-destruct is not the most attractive. But where to start?

If this is Dr Hoffmann's doing, then you imagine that none of this is here by chance. Is there a way to get that key out of the box? And is there anything else hidden somewhere in the room that might work as a code of sorts?

57

A vase containing a few flowers. Some petals have fallen, but the flowers look in fine condition, and are clearly well watered.

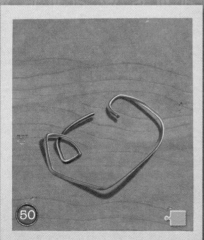

50

This flexible copper wire is the only bit of debris in the room. Dr Hoffmann must run a fairly tight ship here.

STOP HERE! To re-examine the reception room, return to the pages numbered 6.

You wander over to the electrical panel, which is now humming with energy. You are sure you are meant to flick some of the pins on, to activate... whatever it activates. But which ones?

The code from the microscope has colours that match the colours on the electrical panel. But what do the numbers refer to?

To complete this panel, you may now add Red 9 (1+7+1) to a Blue number.

Ah, now you understand, they refer to which pins to switch on the panel! The fourth, third and fourth, working down from the top.

You can also re-examine the generator room on the pages numbered 92 or the reception room on the pages numbered 6.

You decide to search the generator room diligently, to ensure that you have not missed anything. Your training does not allow for shoddy workmanship.

You are quickly glad that you did, because you spot something glinting in the corner.

On the floor, you spot a small glass slide. It might not be anything at all, but you pocket it carefully, just in case it is useful later.

You now have A SMALL GLASS SLIDE and may add Blue 7 to a Red number. You can continue exploring the generator room by turning to the pages numbered 92, or return to the reception room by turning to the pages numbered 6.

You approach the poster and peer through the glass slide at it, hoping some hidden text will reveal itself. No… just a poster. You feel foolish.

Add a penalty to your notebook and return to the pages numbered 6 to continue your search.

The key you retrieved from the box fits perfectly in the lock for the generator room. Finally, you have found a way out of this room! You enter a new space, which is almost completely filled by a large generator. That checks out. At the back of the room, there are a few pieces of furniture, as well as some other objects dotted around. It's time to explore again. You turn to your right, away from the generator.

You see some sort of electrical panel with 12 pins. It seems to have no power, once again. However, there are a series of numbers taped onto it for some reason.

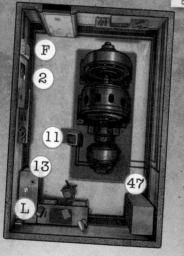

A poster of the Solar System. It's probably not too surprising to see something like this in a laboratory. He is a man of science, after all. And underground lairs are notorious for hiding views of the night sky.

There is still plenty more to look at in this room, but you are already intrigued. The puzzling situation is of such interest that you are almost starting to forget the time pressure on you. You must press on!

To continue exploring the generator room, turn to the pages numbered 13. You can also return to the reception room by turning to the pages numbered 6.

You look around and your attention is grabbed by a filing cabinet in the back corner of the room, which was previously hidden by the generator. There must be something of interest in there! Perhaps the Formula?

As is becoming a pattern, the filing cabinet is locked. You are stymied. The lock indicates there must be something worthwhile inside.

You backtrack across the room and see a scrap of paper left loose on the table. Does Hoffmann doodle in his spare time?

There is still plenty more to look at in this room, but you are already intrigued. The puzzling situation is of such interest that you are almost starting to forget the time pressure on you. You must press on!

The generator appears to be off, but there is a keypad next to it that must be the way to activate it and get some power going.

Aha, a projector slide. You just had the feeling that Dr Hoffmann would be just the sort of person that would like to give slide shows.

STOP HERE! You can return to the reception room by turning to the pages numbered 6, or re-examine the generator room by returning to the pages numbered 92.

TO CHECK TO SEE IF YOU ENTERED THE CORRECT CODE, TURN TO PAGE 218 AT THE BACK OF THE BOOK.

The generator begins to rumble, and you can hear power begin to flow. You hope that you have not accidentally returned power to the self-destruct mechanism. You suppose you will find out soon enough!

To your relief, you appear to have entered the code correctly the first time! Paying attention in math class pays off once more.

The generator starts up.

If you guessed the wrong code, take a penalty. You are now able to add Blue 15 to a Red number. You can also use the electrical panel, but you'll need to find the correct page. You can re-examine the generator room on the pages numbered 92 and the reception room on the pages numbered 6.

13

There is surely only one place to use this projector slide. You hurry back into the other room, and eagerly insert it. What will it reveal – the hidden Formula? You pray it is not a picture from Dr Hoffmann's last holiday.

LAB

25

The wall opposite the projector lights up. A hidden door! And clearly, the way into the lab. You can't figure out how to open it yet, though.

12

You can continue examining the reception room by turning to the pages numbered 6, or return to the generator room by turning to the pages numbered 92.

No amount of bashing the
control panel will help. Nothing
is happening. You have to add
something else to the panel in order
to make it work.

Add a penalty to your notebook and return to the pages numbered 6 to continue your search.

H

THE FORMULA

TO CHECK TO SEE IF YOU ENTERED THE CORRECT CODE, TURN TO PAGE 218 AT THE BACK OF THE BOOK.

You are baffled by the noises you are hearing. If this is what Dr Hoffmann listens to while he works, you are quite happy that you never met him. However, as you listen you start to think that you can make out a pattern in the sounds. Yes, perhaps you just got it the wrong way around.

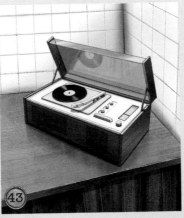

43

You reset the dials to the correct numbers. The voice calls out again: "To open the safe, add eleven." Clear as mud, you think.

If you guessed the wrong numbers, take a penalty. To look around the lab again, return to the pages numbered 56. You can also return to the reception room on the pages numbered 6 and the generator room on the pages numbered 92.

THE FORMULA

31

You follow the instructions Hoffmann left you, and work the control panel. With the generator on, you know that you can count on its added power to help.

B

IT WORKS. YOU HEAR A CLICK NEARBY. +31

31

It works! You hear a click and a creak nearby, like something was opening. Time to investigate.

You may now add Blue 31 to a Red number. Return to the pages numbered 6.

K

The switch on the right gives 2, pressing the black button four times gives 4 and pressing the red button twice gives 10, for a total of 16.

Re-tracing your steps, you check each object with more care – as if your life depended on spotting something you had missed before. It is difficult to stay calm. Suddenly, with a rush of adrenalin you are not sure is entirely healthy, you notice a sign that your eyes had glanced over before. There, on the lab coat…

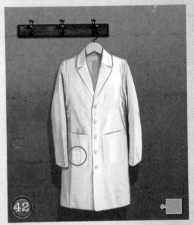

It is faint, but now that you have seen it, you wonder how you missed it with your first sweep: 33, imprinted right on the pocket.

You reach into the pocket with some trepidation. You feel something cool, metal. A key! Never have you felt quite so relieved.

You now have THE COAT KEY and can add Blue 33 to a Red number. Return to the pages numbered 6.

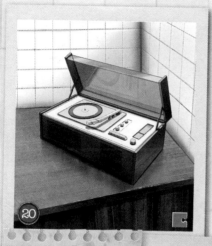

Leaving the vials of liquid where they are for the moment, you take the record over to the player. At the very least, you will have something to listen to while you think. And if you *are* going to die here, then it would be nice to hear music one last time before you do.

As you place the record onto the turntable, you notice that 1234 is written on the label.

You set the dials to 1234 and a strange voice calls out: "... ddaefasehtnepoot." Something isn't right here.

Once you have the correct code, enter it in your notebook then turn to the page labelled H. You can also return to the reception room by turning to the pages numbered 6 or the generator room by turning to the pages numbered 92.

No! This is the wrong letter.
You spend valuable time reading
through Hoffmann's records of his
jam-making.

Hoffmann
Home-Mad

To set,
the rigl
of acid
High-ac
include
cherrie
apples
raspbe
plums.
fruits
juice
pH.

m

needs
alance
pectin.
ruits
rus,
green
neapple,
s and
using other
dd lemon
change the

Add a double penalty to your notebook and return to the pages numbered 85.

No! Why on earth did you run back to the generator when the phone started ringing? Your nerves must be frayed.

Add a penalty to your notebook and
return to the pages numbered 6.

You take the key and start trying to
jam it into any hole in the projector
that you can find. Alas, that's not
how projectors work.

Add a penalty to your notebook and
return to the pages numbered 6.

You stand perplexed for a number of minutes, looking back and forth at everything that you have so far discovered. There are no codes, no keys… what is your next move? The Mona Lisa stares back at you, impassive. Suddenly, a thought strikes you. It may be a long shot, but at the moment it is your only shot.

The last time you came across some artwork in this lab, the word – or rather, the letters – were of utmost importance. Perhaps it is in this case as well?

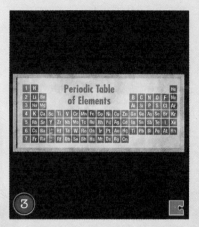

You can spell out Mo-Na-Li-Sa with the elements! And they each give a number: Mo = 5, Na = 3, Li = 2 and Sa = 7.

5-3-2-7. The padlock springs open with a tug. You swing the heavy door of the chest open, eager to see what is inside.

The first thing that catches your eye is a single LP record. Unmarked, so you can't see what it is exactly.

However, something holds you back. Can you be sure this is the Formula? You suspect it is, but you have to be certain. The Formula was somehow meant to assist in your escape. In which case, how do these vials help? They do look like the same type of liquid as those in the medicine cabinet.

93

But, with some glee, you also notice a series of vials filled with an unknown liquid. You want to gather them up as soon as possible.

If you guessed the wrong code, take a penalty. You can return to the reception room by turning to the pages numbered 6 or the generator room by turning to the pages numbered 92, or look around the lab again by turning to the pages numbered 56.

1	H			
2	Li	Be		
3	Na	Mg		
4	K	Ca	Sc	Ti
5	Rb	Sr	Y	Zr
6	Cs	Ba	La-Lu	Hf
7	Fr	Ra	Ac-Lr	Rf

You look around and see that the hidden door concealing the lab has sprung open. Success! If the Formula is anywhere, it must be in there. Eagerly, you leap over to it and rush inside. The lab is much as you would expect it to be: relatively clean, but cluttered, giving the clear feel of being a workplace for a top scientist.

There is much to sort through, and you must do it quickly. First you must decide what is normal for a laboratory, and what might be of interest to you.

(74)

Your eye is drawn to the large safe. When you try it, it's locked, just like everything else in this place. However, this has given you a target. Surely, you need to gain access to it. Unless Hoffmann has left it as a red herring?

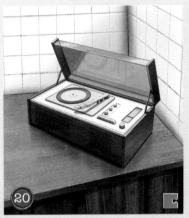

(20)

In the far corner is a record player. There is no record in place. You wonder what Dr Hoffmann likes to listen to while he works? Something calming, no doubt.

You shake yourself out of the reverie you have briefly fallen into while considering the musical tastes of this scientist on whom you are now relying to guide you to the Formula. You *must* stay focused, at all costs. You look around. There is still much to explore in here.

mL
±5%

0 ——— 250
50 ——— 200

— 250
— 200
— 150
— 100

250 ——— 0

To continue exploring the lab, turn to the pages numbered 2. You can also return to the reception room on the pages numbered 6 and the generator room on the pages numbered 92.

You backtrack across the room glancing quickly at the various test tubes and other scientific instruments left out on the work bench. You hope that you aren't meant to focus on his experiments because science was never your strong suit, and you have no idea what any of it means!

As you pass by the end of his work station, you do see something that you recognise at last, tacked on to Hoffmann's wall.

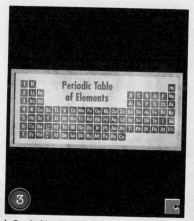

A Periodic Table of elements. What a surprise to see that in a lab! He is not one for wall decorations as a rule, so perhaps this has a function.

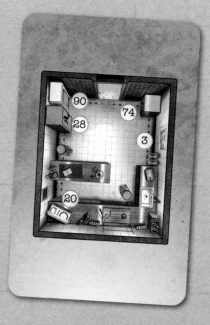

You walk across the room to a closed medicine cabinet made with what looks like… yes… bulletproof glass. But it is unlocked for once!

Next to it is a chest that looks to
be made of reinforced metal from
the size and heft of it. At least
it is nicely decorated.

So, the lab has revealed a series
of extra locks for you to somehow
get past, and a reproduction of the
Mona Lisa. You have to assume that
Dr Hoffmann has left clues to defeat
them. He has brought you this far –
it would seem pointless for him to
abandon you now… to your fate!
But you don't want to think about
that.

And what are those vials in the
medicine cabinet?

On the chest, there's a padlock.
Of course there's a padlock. There
always seems to be a lock in this
place! Hoffmann was clearly not
very trusting.

Open the padlock to
progress. Once you have
the code, turn to the page
labelled M. You can also
return to the reception
room by turning to the
pages numbered 6 or the
generator room by turning
to the pages numbered 92.

No! This is the wrong letter and you have wasted time just to find out that Hoffmann was a keen amateur palaeontologist.

M. W. de

In 1956,
de Laub
publish
suggest
the din
were d
extinc
meteor
Others
at hin
he mi
somet
him A

enfels
N.
s
paper
hat
's
to
by a
mpact.
shed
I think
e on to
Contact

Add a double penalty to your note-book and return to the pages num-bered 85.

For a mad moment, you pick up
the copper wire and try to coax the
projector to life with it. You aren't quite
sure what you are trying to achieve.
This is what panic can do to you.

Add a penalty to your notebook and return to the pages numbered 6 to continue your search.

You can tell flicking those switches has worked – the whole panel is positively humming with power now. But how to harness it? You feel in your pocket for which objects you have left, and the end of the copper wire pricks your finger. You take it out and look at it sceptically.

Copper is a great conductor, and it is just the right length to twist around those three pins. But you don't like the idea of a heart-stopping electrical jolt either. After a minute spent frantically trying to come up with a better plan, you wrap your hand up with your shirt as best you can, and prepare to tie the wire onto the panel.

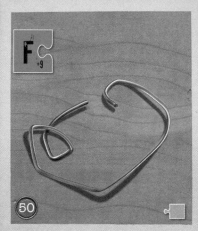

F
+9

50

It sparks, and you wrench your hand away in what seems like the nick of time. You only receive a small jolt. It still stings, though.

RIING!
RIING! THE PHONE
HAS STARTED RINGING!

+27

59

You may now add Blue 27 to a Red number. Return to the pages numbered 6.

Now the generator is on, you need to find something with levers and buttons. You search your memory banks and remember the control panel. You hustle over to it as quickly as possible, acutely aware of the time still ticking away.

This is Hoffmann...
I confess I'm running away,
I can no longer cope with my
terrible discovery.
However, I value human life
and I can't let you die here.
You can only get out with the
formula. Then I'll leave you to
decide the fate of humanity.

To access my lab you must first
turn on the generator. Next,
turn the lever on the right
completely to the right,
press 4 times on the black
button and then, twice on the red.

Good luck.

Y

His instructions are clear enough
- in their own way - now that you
know what he is referring to.

B

The panel not only has a supply,
but there are numbers taped here
that weren't there before. How
did...? Not worth thinking about.

Correctly operating this panel will provide a Red number. You can also return to the reception room on the pages numbered 6 and the generator room on the pages numbered 92.

The shrill tone of the telephone is jarring, after you have been so long in silence. You jump, and you are glad nobody is there to see you so startled by a telephone.

You reach for the receiver and pick up, hardly giving thought to the all-important question of who will be on the other end.

To progress, you must write down the correct code in your notebook and then turn to the page labelled Y. You can also return to the reception room on the pages numbered 6 and the generator room on the pages numbered 92.

A recorded female voice begins to speak immediately: "You have a message, enter your 4-digit security code." But what code?

You have taken to inserting every key in your possession into every lock you come across. Normally, they remain unyielding, but on this occasion you are excited to feel movement and hear a more-than-satisfying click!

You now have AN ULTRAVIOLET LAMP (Blue 80). Return to the pages numbered 92.

The cabinet is almost empty… how disappointing. You are just turning away when, in the top drawer, you find what looks like an ultraviolet lamp.

You return to the reception room and look around, somewhat at a loss for what your next step should be. You are certain, though, that if you look closely enough you will find your next step. And you realise that is exactly what you should be doing! Looking as closely as you can – through the microscope – at the glass slide.

7

You peer once more at what looks like a plain glass slide. Well, we will see, you think, as you position it under the microscope.

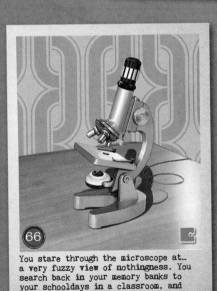

66

You stare through the microscope at... a very fuzzy view of nothingness. You search back in your memory banks to your schooldays in a classroom, and remember how to focus it.

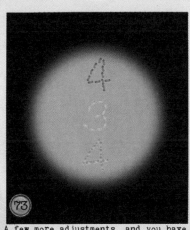

A few more adjustments, and you have
it! On the plate, you see a tiny
inscription. There is simply no
chance that this can be a coincidence.
Someone went to great lengths to hide
this from you.

Or, perhaps, to reveal it to you?
You are beginning to feel
that this whole set-up is
somewhat contrived, as if
someone is leaving clues
to lead you in a certain
direction. But who is doing the
leading? And where are you being
led? You shake your head. These are
questions for another time, when
you aren't in a self-destructing room.

You may return to the reception room on the pages numbered 6 or
the generator room on the pages numbered 92.

You try to dangle the wire into the box, but no. The wire is much too short to catch the key. That was not one of your better ideas, and you have just wasted precious time.

Add a penalty to your notebook and
return to the pages numbered 6 to
continue your search.

You pass the UV lamp over the
poster, expecting to see some
hidden message. Beyond the
mysteries of the cosmos, there
is nothing.

Add a penalty to your notebook and
return to the pages numbered 92.

There must be some other way to get at the key in the box, other than brute force. If you're honest, you would be happy if brute force would work, but in this instance it has been of no use to you. It is time to engage the brain.

The seconds tick by as you ponder, your eyes flicking ever more incessantly between the objects until – EUREKA! Your discovery might not be quite as profound as the original *eureka* moment was, but it has the potential to be just as life-changing, for you at least.

57

The well-tended flowers were almost drowning in water. You felt sure that they could spare some of it for you.

27

You tip the water from the vase into the box and watch in delight as the cork rises with the water level.

Now that you have a key, you begin to feel a lot better. Hardly thinking, you rush to try it in the hatch – no luck. Escape will not be that easy. You begin to worry that this was only the beginning.

84

The cork is quickly within reach, and you pull it out of the box with the key firmly attached to it.

You now have THE VASE KEY and may add Blue 84 to a Red number. Return to the pages numbered 6.

You now have the message, and the safe has been intriguing you ever since you first entered the room. You had assumed the Formula was inside it, but if the Formula is the liquid in the vials, then what could possibly be in the safe?

You check your watch. Time is getting very short and you can't afford to waste any more of it, so you tell yourself to stop wondering and find out. You hurry over to the safe.

You bend down to examine the opening mechanism. Add 11… you are no locksmith or bank robber, but you think you have it.

It's open and contains a small filing
cabinet. You stare aghast at the
files. Are you now meant to find the
Formula in amongst all this junk?

You assume that you need
Hoffmann's workings. Even if those
liquids are the Formula, without
knowing how to re-create it the vials
will be close to worthless. But you
have just minutes left, and there are
thousands of papers here. You are a
quick reader, but this is beyond you.

You could just take everything,
but not only would it be very heavy,
you assume that the information
you need to escape is hidden
somewhere in there. Where to
begin? You are determined not to
panic. There has to be a way to
narrow the files down to just
one letter.

To progress, you must turn
to the correct letter. You will
receive a double penalty for
making an incorrect guess.
You also can return to the
reception room on the pages
numbered 6, the generator
room on the pages numbered
92 and look around the lab
again by turning to the pages
numbered 56.

No! This is the wrong letter and all you have learned is that Hoffmann has a weird obsession with snakes. You can't worry about that right now.

Reasons
Purchas

Snakes
fascina
compan
Snakes
requir
walks
With
defec
snake
also
up.

Add a double penalty to your notebook and return to the pages numbered 85.

ke

ake

ets.
ot
ly
e park.
quent
, a pet
bitat is
sy clean-

You aren't quite sure what you are looking for, but at this point every lead is worth chasing down. You switch the lights off in the room, and you are instantly plunged into darkness. Creepy. This far underground, it's absolutely pitch black. You don't like it…

80

You turn on the UV lamp and you are bathed in a cold blue glow. You start to walk around the room slowly, searching every object with care.

11

As you approach the generator, you notice a glow coming from the keypad! There are marks there that weren't there before.

You have found fingerprint marks
(someone must have very dirty
fingers), and some odd symbols
as well.

You now have a good idea of the four numbers that could turn the generator on, but how do you know the order? You are – quite justifiably, given your situation – concerned that the generator could be booby-trapped, and any incorrect input might cause… well… more trouble than you are already in.

There must be a way to get this right the first time. You switch the light back on and settle down to think. What were those symbols? They seem familiar. You search back, and think you recognise them from your school days. Hmmm…

With some trepidation, you approach the keypad and enter four numbers.

To progress, you must write down the correct code in your notebook and then turn to the page labelled K.

A code… a code… you've run out of codes, haven't you? Thinking back, you can't remember any other numbers or colours that you have found dotted around the room. You furiously search the objects you have discovered, and find nothing there either.

Nothing, that is, until you find the small scrap of paper that had been left on the table. It is then that you notice the small image imprinted next to the phone's dialler.

(L)

It may or may not be a doodle, but it is clearly a wing. You need four numbers, and the word "WING" contains four letters.

(64)

Using the phone's dialler, you can translate WING into four numbers. W = 9, I = 4, N = 6, G = 4. You enter the numbers.

This is Hoffmann...

I confess I'm running away,
I can no longer cope with my
terrible discovery.

However, I value human life
and I can't let you die here.
You can only get out with the
formula. Then I'll leave you to
decide the fate of humanity.

To access my lab you must first
turn on the generator. Next,
turn the lever on the right,
completely to the right,
press 4 times on the black
button and then, twice on the red.

Good luck.

The voice of the person who you
assume to be Dr Hoffmann comes on
the line. His message explains some
things, but is rather cryptic.

Well, it appears that you getting out of this underground lab will not just determine your fate, but also that of the entire world. Your heart sinks, even as your adrenalin spikes and your mind clears.

Your training has taught you to focus entirely on one thing at a time, and your objectives are still clear. First, find the Formula. Second, make your escape. Third… you can cross that bridge if you ever make it that far.

If you guessed the wrong code, take a penalty. If you have already turned on the generator, turn to the page labelled R. Otherwise, you must return to the pages numbered 92, and once you have turned on the generator you can turn to the page labelled R.

You inspect the key minutely through the microscope, but it is just a key. You're not sure what you expected to find.

Add a penalty to your notebook and
return to the pages numbered 6.

As you are staring bewildered at the files in front of you, a voice interrupts your thoughts. "Self-destruct in five minutes. I repeat: five minutes." You start to flick through the files frantically, before you slow down and force yourself to focus. What could these letters mean? Is there anything remaining in these rooms that has appeared unusual or not been useful yet?

Dr Hoffmann is a man of logic, and so far he has led you from location to location expertly. He would not leave the final step to chance. You close your eyes, and see black. And that's when it hits you. You rush into the generator room, just as the voice booms out: "Four minutes."

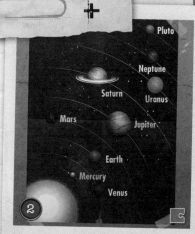

The letters match the names of the planets in the Solar System, except for one. It has to be Neptune. N for Neptune!

You rush back, and flip to the folder labelled N. And there it is - the Formula, at last. And now, to the exit. No time to lose!

71 The door remains as firmly locked as ever. "Three minutes," comes the voice. You turn to the keypad next to the door.

19 Well, this is it. The final test. Can you figure out the code? Your mind is blank and - "Two minutes." - you need it to find the answer one final time!

That voice, that voice! It has begun a second-by-second count now. 104… 103… 102… You have the many vials in your backpack and held awkwardly under one arm… 98… 97… 96… and the Formula clutched in the other hand. Think, think, think! You now have 80 seconds left.

Can you enter the correct code in time?

To escape the lab, you must enter the right code in your notebook and turn to the page labelled C. You will receive a <u>triple</u> penalty for making an incorrect guess. You can also explore the reception room on the pages numbered 6, the generator room on the pages numbered 92 and the lab on the pages numbered page 56 and M.

The Formula must help you escape. You scan it as quickly as you can, but you're no chemist. The scientific notations mean nothing to you. It may as well be written in Russian for all the good it does you. Is this truly it? 55... 54.... 53... Undone by the lack of a doctorate in molecular chemistry?

N

Wait - four numbers are picked out in colour. The same colours as on the keypad! They must be the numbers you need. But in what order?

93

90

The Formula will help! The colours of the Formula match as well. You quickly count the vials in your possession. "25... 24...."

19

1 grey, 2 blue, 3 red, 4 green. The order! With shaking hands, you stab the keypad: 8-5-6-3. A click next to you.

71

The door swings open as the voice begins to count from 10. You sweep up the vials and rush for the exit.

You run out with the Formula, slamming the heavy metallic door shut with a thud, which is quickly echoed by another – far louder – thud. You don't want to know what the rooms look like now. All you can do is take deep breaths of the warm New York subway air, which never tasted so good.

You look down. A scrap of paper and an armful of vials. It doesn't look like much for something with the potential to change the world. It was too much for Hoffmann, and now the burden rests on you.

Should you hand it over to the authorities – your bosses – or should you destroy it? The choice will be yours. Lost in thought, you escape into the open air.

Congratulations! Turn to page 218 to see your final score!

PENALTIES (X):

ROOM PAGES:

RED NUMBER (OBJECT): **BLUE NUMBER (OBJECT):**

CODES:

OTHER NOTES:

Blasted Professor Noside! Once again, your old enemy has conjured up an evil plan that it is up to you to thwart, and you have courageously slipped into his headquarters to discover and prevent it. While you wander through the corridors of the old shack that serves as his HQ, a trap door opens beneath your feet and you find yourself in a terrifying – but fortunately short – fall into a dark and damp dungeon.

Your screams will not help you: you're a prisoner of the professor, and it's very scary... hence the screams. The world is lost forever, unless you can somehow get out of here and sabotage the plans of Noside.

You are the world's last hope. You can't fail.

You are plunged into darkness!
Oh dear. And screaming is still
not helpful in the slightest.
Perhaps it's time to stop that.
Go no further until you figure
out a solution to your
opaque ordeal!

When you solve the puzzle, turn to the correct page.

You certainly aren't going to ruin the cupcakes with this cheddar. In fact, given the strong smell coming from it, you think that this has the capability of ruining a cheddar cheese sandwich. If Noside actually enjoys this, he is even more twisted than you thought.

It might not be fit for human consumption, but you think your newfound friend would love it. You once caught a mouse gnawing your underwear, so you don't think they are too choosy.

32

20

Lured by the cheese, the mouse
comes out of the hole. You have
difficulty catching it but after
some ungainly dives, you succeed in
the end. Hooray!

The mouse is adorable and nervous,
so you introduce yourself and
explain that you're not one of
Noside's henchmen. Then you
suddenly remember that you don't
know the rodent's name, so you ask
politely. It duly responds: "Squeek!"
This sounds a bit cliché, so you
decide to call the mouse James.

You can revisit the rest of the kitchen by turning to
the pages numbered **57**. You can also return to the
Storeroom on the pages numbered **1** and the HQ on the
pages labelled **F**.

Now that you've rewound the tape, it's time to see what's on there. Please be *Titanic*, please be *Titanic*. There's nothing you like better than seeing Jack slowly sinking while you know that there was room on that door for both of them. So selfish, Rose.

The despicable Professor Noside appears... "You're at my mercy!" I will **destroy this planet** and no-one, not even you, can stop my evil plan!" Cheery, as always.

He's just begging to be taken down a peg or two, isn't he? Especially considering that his dastardly scheme consists in part of locking you in a storeroom with two VCRs. Even so, the sight of his evil visage and maniacal **laugh** takes the breath from your lungs. For just a moment it feels like the world has **turned upside down**. You – yes, you – are going to stop his evil plan. Somehow. And, in fact, you think he has just given you the code you need.

To return to the Storeroom, turn to the pages numbered **1**.

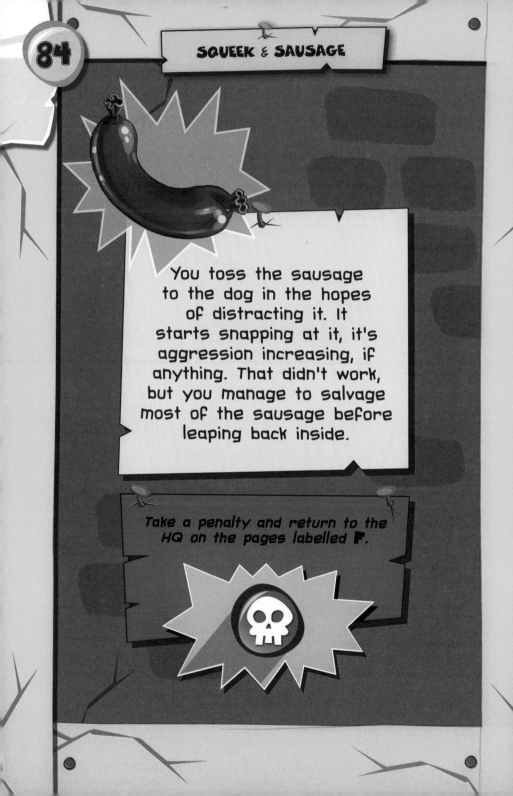

You toss the sausage to the dog in the hopes of distracting it. It starts snapping at it, it's aggression increasing, if anything. That didn't work, but you manage to salvage most of the sausage before leaping back inside.

Take a penalty and return to the HQ on the pages labelled **F**.

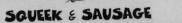

James enters the maze through hole **9**. He refuses to move, and climbs back out of the hole moments later. Your budding friendship is fraying already.

Take a penalty and return to the maze on the pages numbered **100**.

Who could be after that cheese? You wouldn't exactly call it appetising. Then again anyone who thinks choc-cheese is a good combination must have some odd tastes.

Performing a final sweep of the room, you notice a small hole in the wall that you'd not noticed before. Noside is spending too much money on cooks, and not enough on maintenance.

A mouse hole. Perhaps you'd even call it a mouse home.

You can just spy a mouse, shuddering in the dark. You want to coax it out but realise you don't know its name. Do mice have names? You shrug. Instead, you tell it of your plan to take down Professor Noside and achieve undying glory. It remains unconvinced. You think you will become firm friends.

You can return to the Kitchen by turning to the pages numbered **57**. You may also revisit the Storeroom on the pages numbered **1** and the HQ on the pages labelled **F**.

SQUEEK & SAUSAGE

Oh. That was easier than expected. Well, maybe you'll get a sandwich named after you. That would be nice. You blink in the sudden light until your eyes re-adjust. Time to take a look around at the horrors that lie in store.

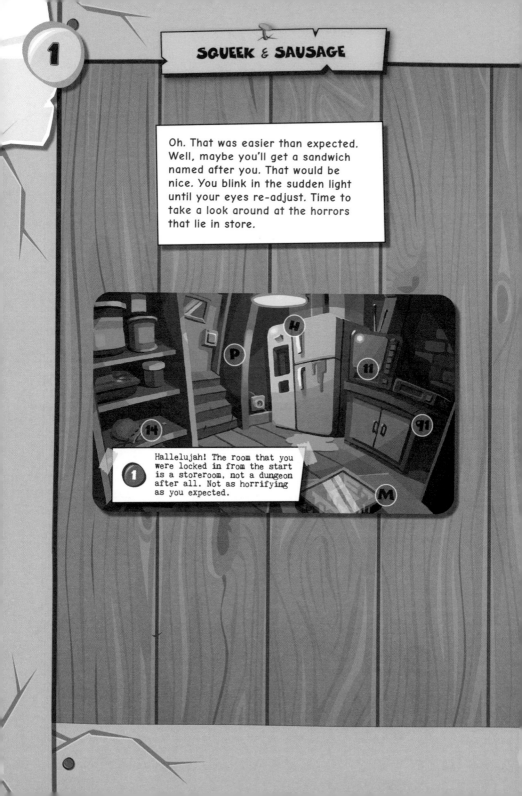

1 Hallelujah! The room that you were locked in from the start is a storeroom, not a dungeon after all. Not as horrifying as you expected.

This door is locked with a digital code. If only Y2K could strike right now, that would be sweet. When you have the 4-digit code for the locked door, turn to the pages labelled F.

This appears to be part of a puzzle. Amazing. Because it's a... you get the idea. It seems pretty useless right now.

You swallow your disappointment at the locked door – and your fright at seeing Noside staring out at you – and start looking around the room.. If you're unable to escape then this will be your new home. You wonder what the wi-fi reception is like.

To continue exploring the Storeroom, turn to the pages labelled H.

A high-tech refrigerator. It makes ice in different shapes. The instructions are simple: add water. Choose the shape of your ice. Enjoy!

A bag containing strange little seeds. Mighty oaks from little acorns grow, they say, but you don't have that kind of time.

Seeds and a refrigerator? This storeroom is pretty tricked out, you think to yourself. Does Professor Noside spend a lot of time here or does he have a horde of henchmen making him novelty ice cubes at all hours of the night? You spot a note left next to the fridge. It says: to use the star shape, add red 35 to a blue number attached to an object. To use the skull shape, add red 30 to the blue number and to use the heart shape, add red 47 to the blue number.

11

An ancient TV/VCR combo. This probably cost Professor Noside a fortune back in the day, and now look at it.

91

A dilapidated old VCR. Who knows why someone would own both a TV/ VCR combo and a VCR recorder, but then Noside is a notorious madman.

You've come to the end of your storeroom tour. You suppose that an open window and a sandwich was too much to hope for. The seeds won't fill you up much. There must be a way through that door, or at least something good to watch on TV. You squint at the blank screen. It doesn't help, but it does give you an idea.

Stop here! To revisit the first part of the Storeroom, return to the pages numbered **1**.

Well, you don't have much else to do other than explore what Noside has locked in his desk. He needs a better filing system. If he wasn't so outright evil, you would tell him where the nearest stationer's is.

Some papers marked with a number 4 fall out of the green folder as you are rifling through. Worth a closer look, you think.

THANK YOU FOR PURCHASING
THE MYKKIMAZE™ RODENT MAZE.

TO ENJOY IT, START BY FIXING
THE PARTS OF THE MAZE TOGETHER.

THEN SLIP YOUR FAVOURITE RODENT
IN THE RIGHT HOLE AND WATCH
HIM HAPPILY ROMP AROUND.

WHAT FUN FOR YOU AND YOUR SMALL
PET! IF HE FINDS THE CORRECT PATH, A
WELL-DESERVED REWARD
WILL BE RELEASED.

4

Assembly instructions for a
Swedish toy kit. Fortunately, their
knowledge of English is impeccable
so you don't need to translate it.

Of course Noside would have his
own personal rodent maze. You
can just imagine the hours of
unhinged delight he must have as
he watches his next tiny victim
scramble around. It's probably
where he got the idea for this
ordeal. It's just that you're
slightly bigger and you're less
interested in cheese.

You can return to the Desk by turning to the pages
numbered 9. You can also revisit the HQ on the pages
labelled F, the Storeroom on the pages numbered 1 and
the Kitchen on the pages numbered 57.

You want to give the seeds the best chance in life. And you don't have much else going on right now... so you decide to water them. You'll have to get this pipe system to work first though.

It all fits! The pipes have numbers etched into them too, and they add up to 16.

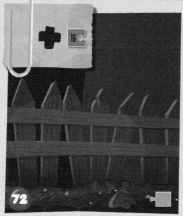

72

88

Oooooooooooooooh! The flowers grow instantly. Both a magical and a beautiful show. Very unexpected.

They're unlike any flowers you've ever seen. Perhaps Noside has been dabbling with some genetic engineering?

You can revisit the rest of the Garden by turning to the pages numbered **51** or return to the Kitchen on the pages numbered **57**, the Storeroom on the pages numbered **1** and the HQ on the pages labelled **F**.

You put your new friend James into the hole marked with a *16*. He wanders around aimlessly. You know the feeling...

Take a penalty and return to the maze on the pages numbered *100*.

Your heart's
not really in this,
is it?

Take a penalty and return to the
page you just came from.

You grope in the dark and end up finding... Yes! This feels like a switch.

You peer at it and can just about make out two numbers stamped into the plastic casing. What can they mean?

You mustn't proceed until you crack this fiendish puzzle. It will take all of your cunning, all of your skill. It demands your tenacity, your audacity, your perspicacity, but, oh, it will be worth it. They will write epic poems about this day. Schools will be retitled in tribute to you, and streets, and mid-sized community centres. An actor will win an Oscar for putting on a fake nose and playing you. A generation of children will be named after you, and the one after that. Solving this will be a triumph for the ages.

When you solve the puzzle, turn to the correct page number.

You lean back on your chair, contemplating the life choices that got you to this moment. You tip too far and almost fall, catching yourself and thanking your luck that there was nobody here to see it except for the viciously cute guard dog. As you right yourself, you catch sight of a pattern on the doormat.

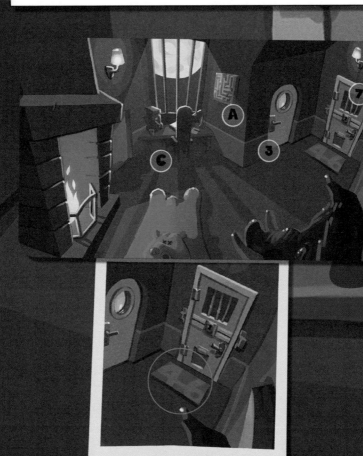

The number 46. Cautiously, you approach. There had better not be another trapdoor underneath it.

You look under the doormat and find a KEY! You can now add Blue 46 to a red number. Fancy that.

What brings down an evil genius? Overconfidence, usually, which manifests itself as carelessness. They're always so convinced of their own superior intellect that they fail to tie up every loose end. Sometimes they even leave a key under a doormat. Does Professor Noside really think so little of you?

To continue exploring the HQ, turn to the pages labelled **F**. You can also return to the Storeroom on the pages numbered **1**.

You insert the skull-shaped icy pole into the door and hope for the best. It works! This is the peril of not using regular locks.

54

3

57 You enter the kitchen and take a look around. It's surprisingly homely. Does Noside do his own cooking?

63

A cupboard shut with a combination lock. It contains cheese. And flies. Who would want to break in?? When you have the code for the combination lock, turn to the page numbered 32. Time is ticking.

E

It's the final part of the maze. Finally!

You lay all four pieces of the maze on the kitchen table, briefly befuddled. What a rat run this is. Turn to the pages numbered 100 to see it fit all together.

*To continue exploring the Kitchen, turn to the pages numbered 41. You can also return to the Storeroom on the pages numbered 1 and the HQ on the pages labelled F.*

41

A poster of questionable taste decorates the decrepit wall. Mesmerising.

You wonder if it's a magic eye thing or if Noside is just really into squid. Are squid evil? They seem more evil than a haddock, say, but you understand that this prejudice is entirely irrational. You stare at the poster a little longer, slack-jawed, your eyes glazing over. Time to move on, but perhaps it will be of some use.

89

It's an oven in which some cupcakes are baking. You hope Noside has a timer on. They look delicious, but you wouldn't trust anything he's baked. A message is stuck on the door.

DEAR PROFESSOR,

HERE ARE THE CHOC-CHEDDAR CUPCAKES YOU ASKED FOR. I'VE GONE TO DO SOME SHOPPING. IF YOU COULD JUST ADD THE CHEESE AT THE RIGHT TIME, IT WOULD HELP ME PS: TO STOP THE CHEDDAR BEING EATEN BY YOU-KNOW-WHO, I'VE LOCKED IT IN THE CUPBOARD. I WON'T GIVE YOU THE CODE, I KNOW YOU LOVE DEDUCTION GAMES. GIVEN YOUR INTELLIGENCE, YOU SHOULDN'T HAVE ANY PROBLEMS GUESSING IT!
PPS: DON'T BURN EVERYTHING LIKE LAST TIME

EDOUIGE

73

Choc-cheddar! The man truly is evil. The message is probably from Noside's cook and it explains a few things. Not the choc-cheddar combination, though.

Who knew that being an evil mastermind would pay well enough to afford a cook to bake you odd little cupcakes. You wonder if you've taken the wrong career path, and shrug it off: this monster must pay.

Stop here! You can revisit the rest of the Kitchen by turning to the pages numbered **57**. *You can also return to the Storeroom on the pages numbered* **1** *and the HQ on the pages labelled* **F**.

Absolutely not. Just think about it for a minute. The stars are not aligning for you.

Take a penalty and return to the page you just came from.

Neither the dog nor the door is interested in the cheese. The dog has better sense and the door... well, it's a door.

Take a penalty and return to the HQ on the pages labelled F.

You'd completely forgotten about that key you found under the doormat. You use it on the door and it opens again. Well, that was incredibly easy. He can remotely close and lock a door, but he can't hide the key more than a metre from it. This man's mind is quite something. This time, thankfully, the loudspeaker remains silent. You step over the snoring dog and approach the shed-laboratory.

A charming little garden, worthy of a house in the suburbs. Does he have a gardener as well as a cook? The man has serious money.

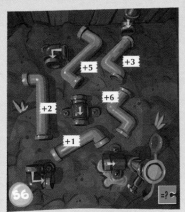

The water inlet pipes have fallen down. You must find the right ones if you want to get the water. Add the correct ones together to make a red number.

A brown substance. Granular and slightly damp. It's... yes! It is! It's soil!

You need to get in: this room contains a weapon of mass destruction. Oh - perhaps you should have mentioned that earlier... yeah, that's his plan. When you have the correct 4-digit code, turn to the pages numbered 36.

Although the garden is charming it could definitely use a little more care and attention. The drainage system could be fixed at the very least. Noside is a busy man, obviously, but perhaps he should spend a little more time on his garden and a little less time on trying to destroy the world.

You can return to the Kitchen by turning to the pages numbered 57, the Storeroom on the pages numbered 1 and the HQ on the pages labelled F.

You feel so clever to have added 30 minutes to 12:17, the precise time that the chef needs to bake the cupcakes before adding the cheddar, added to the start time on the oven. You enter 1247 into the combination lock, open the cupboard and take the cheese that's hidden behind a cloud of flies. If you entered the wrong code, **take a penalty** as well as the cheese.

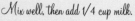

Add 2 eggs and the melted chocolate.

Sift in 4.5oz flour and a pinch of baking powder.

Mix well, then add 1/4 cup milk.

Fill the molds with this delicious mixture and bake for 30 minutes at 300°F.

When almost ready, add the cheddar and continue baking until golden!

78

A small piece of cheddar, matured for 18 months. The best! There's no way you're adding this to the cupcakes.

*You can revisit the rest of the kitchen by turning to the pages numbered **57**. You can also return to the Storeroom on the pages numbered **1** and the HQ on the pages labelled **F**.*

You wonder if the eject button still works on this ancient bit of kit.

A VHS cassette comes out of the video recorder with difficulty. It probably heard about the death of physical media and is terrified, the poor thing.

Your squinting helped you spot the 18 on the VCR but now you can't stop and it's giving you a headache. Apparently this video is of Michel Gondry's 2008 comedy starring Jack Black and Mos Def. While you're trapped here, that'll pass 98 minutes or so.

To return to the Storeroom, turn to the pages numbered 1.

SQUEEK & SAUSAGE

After much deliberating, you decide on a starting point for the maze. You think you've made the right choice, but will the mouse? You gently pop James into the maze through hole number 25.

He takes a bit of time to get going while you shout encouragement at him like you are his personal trainer at a terribly confusing gym.

A sausage. What a glorious prize. It was released when the mouse skittered over the opening button of the maze's trapdoor.

Success! Driven by the scent of the sausage and what you can only assume is a deep love of puzzles, he takes every correct turn. Just as he's about to reach his quarry, however, James the mouse passes over the button and delivers the pork prize to your waiting hands. You almost feel bad for him, but also he's already had some cheese and there's a world to save.

You can return to the Kitchen by turning to the pages numbered **57**, the Storeroom on the pages numbered **1** and the HQ on the pages labelled **F**.

You grab the red book from the drawer and flip through the pages at random. It's disconcerting to think of Noside as being a fan of music, even if that music happened to be ominous and intimidating. He must have other intentions in mind for this music, undoubtedly nefarious ones.

A music score. Tadadadadada dum. It's catchy but you have no idea how to use it.

You can return to the Desk by turning to the pages numbered 9. You can also revisit the HQ on the pages labelled F, the Storeroom on the pages numbered 1 and the Kitchen on the pages numbered 57.

You pour water into the hi-tech ice maker. It rumbles in contemplation for a few moments before producing a single ice cube. You grab a stick from the shelf and now you have a creepy popsicle. They call them icy poles in Australia, what's that about?

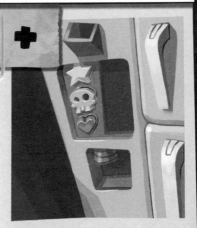

Ice in the shape of a skull. Very pretty.

You can return to the Storeroom on the pages numbered **1** and the HQ on the pages labelled **F**.

53

You put the VHS cassette
in the fridge. You take it
back out a minute later.
It's a bit colder.

Take a penalty and return to the
page you just came from.

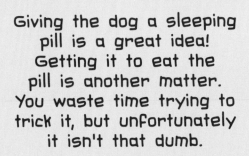

Giving the dog a sleeping
pill is a great idea!
Getting it to eat the
pill is another matter.
You waste time trying to
trick it, but unfortunately
it isn't that dumb.

Take a penalty and return to the
HQ on the pages labelled **F**.

"There's something suspicious about that suspicious laugh!" you exclaim at the television. "Or something even more suspicious than usual, anyway. I can see it on the screen, for one thing." You type 3434 into the door and it creaks open. **If you got the code wrong, take a penalty.**

F
You have entered some sort of strange… study? This must be the real headquarters. There's a desk and everything. Right next to all the dead animals - lovely décor.

Another part of a puzzle. Amaz... Neat.

A note is taped to the door: "Kitchen. Please do not enter." It's hard to argue with such a polite request. You look at the lock and wonder if he had to have it custom-made.

An entrance (and, obviously, an exit - deep stuff). Those are some heavy-duty locking mechanisms. But none of them are in use - freedom!

The door opens onto a pretty garden in the middle of which stands Noside's shed-laboratory. You need to enter! But as you step out an aggressive guard dog comes out of the shadows.

He growls menacingly — it's impossible to get past while this monster is still here! Just look at his mean, strangely adorable little face! You return inside. You must be getting closer: the fire is roaring away. Surely even Professor Noside wouldn't be irresponsible enough to leave a fireplace unattended for too long. Yes, he may want to destroy the planet, but there's always time for fire safety. You contemplate lying out on the rug and warming your weary bones, but there's work to be done and a headquarters to examine.

To continue exploring the HQ, turn to the pages labelled **C**.

You sit down in Professor Noside's chair and look out the window. The desk has a good view of his shed-laboratory.

You can just picture him sitting here cackling away, upside-down numbers pouring out of his mouth.

A tidy desk. It must be here that Noside puts the finishing touches to his evil plans. It all seems very analogue for a criminal mastermind.

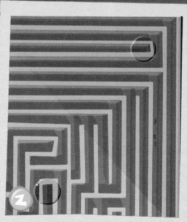

Another part of a maze. What a puzzle this puzzle is.

A simple glass of water. Good for drinking and various other uses.

This drawer is locked because life is never easy. When you have the 4-digit code, turn to the pages numbered 9.

It's not as if you were expecting Professor Noside to leave all of his incriminating evidence spread out across the desk, but there's not a single blueprint to be exploited. Outside, the dog barks, as if it's making fun of you. There must be something else in this room other than a great view and a lovely fire.

Stop here! To revisit the HQ, turn to the pages labelled **H**. You can also return to the Storeroom on the pages numbered **1**.

SQUEEK & SAUSAGE

With some trepidation, you turn to the recipe book. What ingeniously diabolical concoctions will you find in here? Broccoli and liquorice cookies? Jam and ham tarts? Carrot cake? Oh – that one works actually.

You turn swiftly to page 78. Some of the images on the other pages are truly gruesome. Noside's poor cook doesn't deserve this.

Granny Jacquotte's fabulous
choc-cheddar
cupcakes !

◆ Beat 3oz softened butter with 2.5oz sugar.

◆ Add 2 eggs and the melted chocolate.

◆ Sift in 4.5oz flour and a pinch of baking powder.

◆ Mix well, then add 1/4 cup milk.

◆ Fill the molds with this delicious mixture and bake for 30 minutes at 300°F.

◆ When almost ready, add the cheddar and continue baking until golden!

78

The page is for the cupcakes in the oven. You tear it from the book. If you ever get out, it's all the evidence you need that Noside is a lunatic. Time will prove it.

broccoli

Add 2 cups steamed broccoli

Mix with the liquorice

The smell of chocolate wafts over from the oven, finally displacing the extra-mature cheddar. You examine the recipe, trying to make sense of it. Is this a clue? Is Noside just really into cupcakes and wants to keep his favourite recipe safe? It's not the worst idea in the world.

You can return to the Desk by turning to the pages numbered **9**. You can also revisit the HQ on the pages labelled **F**, the Storeroom on the pages numbered **1** and the Kitchen on the pages numbered **57**.

You open the door slightly and carefully throw the sausage into the garden. Noises of something being wolfed down can be heard immediately. After a few seconds, the chewing noises are replaced by deep snores.

7

83

The dog has fallen asleep. You will finally be able to get out... but Noside's voice suddenly comes from a loudspeaker!

90

"You really think it would be so easy and I'd let you go like that?"
Click-Clack

5

The door has swung shut and is now locked! For some reason, the evil professor really does not want you to save the Earth.

A part of you did think it would be so easy and Noside would let you go just like that. You sigh deeply, and James emerges from its hole to see what you're so upset about.

"There's no way an ice cube is going to save me this time", you tell the mouse, but he doesn't really understand what you mean.

You can revisit the HQ on the pages labelled **F** or return to the Kitchen on the pages numbered **57** and the Storeroom on the pages numbered **1**.

SQUEEK & SAUSAGE

The smell of the cupcakes is making you extremely hungry – you've not eaten for nearly three hours now, so you can't be blamed for being ravenous. However, you somehow manage to restrain yourself from chowing down on the sausage that has been laying in a maze for an indeterminate number of weeks, months or years.

6

77

You open the capsule and sprinkle the sleeping pill's contents over the sausage. You also somehow find a tiny version of one of those nightcaps that Ebeneezer Scrooge used to wear. It's so strange, you reflect, that there was once a time when it'd get so cold at night you'd need to sleep in a hat, but you don't really have time to think about that right now. In any case, this sausage is now ready to be visited by assorted phantasms and experience a moral rebirth.

This sausage can send anybody into the arms of Morpheus (Morpheus the dream lord, not Morpheus the character from *The Matrix*, or Morpheus the file-sharing Napster rival from the early 2000s).

You can return to the Kitchen by turning to the pages numbered **57**, the Storeroom on the pages numbered **1** and the HQ on the pages labelled **F**.

Putting it in the fridge somehow had no effect on this retro tape, but there must be something else that could be done to it. You think back to your days kickin' it in the '90s. It's a bit hazy, but you recall one of the most frustrating things about that time...

18

The hours spent rewinding tape, at basically the same speed as watching it! The label would indicate a rewind is in order here. You pray it's not as long as *Lord of the Rings*. Especially not the extended edition.

Success! Only a couple of minutes - it's practically a DVD with that sort of speed. You try to remember the last time you rewound a tape, but nothing comes to mind.

That was pretty clever; now you're wishing that you hadn't fantasized about grand accolades for switching on a light switch. This deserves an all-star tribute concert at least. What next with this rewound cassette? The mind boggles.

To return to the Storeroom, turn to the pages numbered 1.

Yes, of course. Throw the seeds at the door. What a good idea! Carry on like that and you might get out in 2058. Picking up these seeds is going to take some time.

Take a penalty and return to the HQ on the pages labelled **F**.

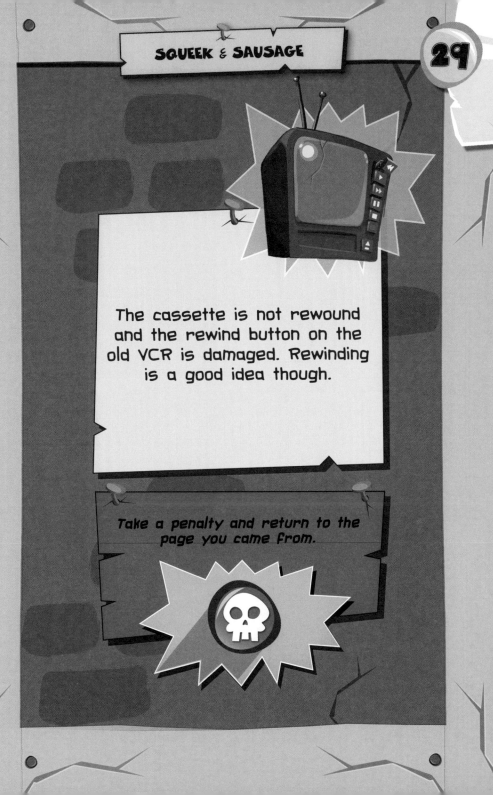

The cassette is not rewound and the rewind button on the old VCR is damaged. Rewinding is a good idea though.

Take a penalty and return to the page you came from.

You take the strange little seeds and plant them. You have had them from the very start, and you are slightly sad to part with them, until you see James peering at you from the doorway. "You're right," you say. "I must plough on." In this case, literally.

14

58

There's nothing quite like gardening to connect you to the Earth you are currently in the process of saving.

Ta-da! The seeds are well planted in the nourishing soil.

It's a shame you won't be around to watch the little guys grow. When this is all over you might send Noside an invoice for all the work you've done around his home.

You can revisit the rest of the Garden by turning to the pages numbered **51** or return to the Kitchen on the pages numbered **57**, the Storeroom on the pages numbered **1** and the HQ on the pages labelled **F**.

Not for the first time in your life, you're glad you decided to count the suckered arms on a weird poster. You enter 7656 into the lock. **If you've guessed the incorrect code, take a penalty.**

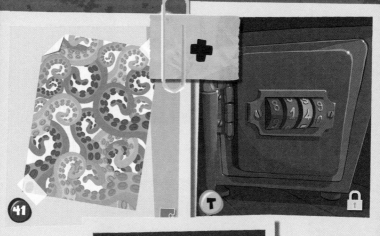

41

T

6

9

The drawer opens silently. It's overflowing with papers and various documents. And… is that a cupcake? The man is obsessed.

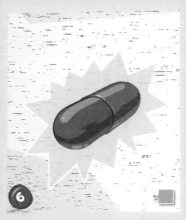

6

A sleeping pill. You prefer
chamomile tea yourself, but it
must be effective or Noside
wouldn't have locked it away.

You rifle through the rest of
the drawer but you have no
idea what else you're trying
to find or where it might be;
Noside has many flaws, and
evidently poor organisation is
among them. You are starting
to feel overwhelmed. Perhaps
a sleeping pill would take the
edge off...

You can explore the HQ again by turning to the pages
labelled **F**. You can also revisit the Storeroom on
the pages numbered **1** and the Kitchen on the pages
numbered **57**.

While the flowers were unlike any you'd ever seen, they **were** arranged just like that musical score you found in the professor's drawer.

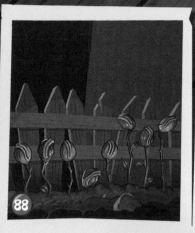

You examine the blue flowers and their positions on the "stave" of the fence. 3-1-5-4. You enter it into the lock and it opens. If you entered the wrong code, **take two penalties.**

Finally, you've made it to Noside's shed-laboratory. You're disappointed to find that he isn't here – presumably he would have heard you mucking around with the inlet pipes in his garden – but there is a cage hanging above you. From your perspective it's impossible to see what's inside,

but it must be critical if Noside has gone to these ridiculous lengths to protect it. You don't really like the skull on the lever mechanism... this seems like it could be a pretty huge decision. You need to get the arrow to point at the "down" icon – not the skull.

A cage is hanging by a chain from the ceiling. Choose the right manoeuvre to get it down:

Push the lever to the left: turn to page G.

OR

-Push the lever to the right: turn to page D.

You can return to the Garden by turning to the pages numbered **51**, the Kitchen on the pages numbered **57**, the Storeroom on the pages numbered **1** and the HQ on the pages labelled **F**.

SQUEEK & SAUSAGE

You now have four pieces of the maze. Counting the corners, you feel pretty sure this is all of them. You haven't spent so much of your adult life putting together jigsaw puzzles for nothing... even if other people tell you that you have. This should be a cinch.

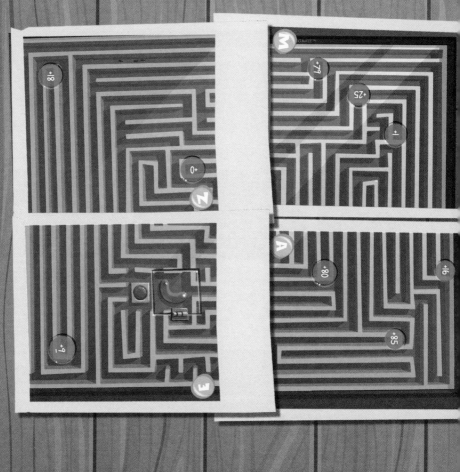

To get the sausage and beat the maze, add the correct red number to... something. Watch out. Some holes might penalize you somehow.

After you put the maze together, you notice numbers marking each entry hole into it. You aren't sure what they mean yet, but you know that you can't wait to get your hands on that sausage.

You can return to the Kitchen by turning to the pages numbered **57**, the Storeroom on the pages numbered **1** and the HQ on the pages labelled **F**.

Rrrrrrrr... You force the lever but it jams the system. You lose time loosening everything up. At least that skull didn't mean *INSTANT DEATH!*

You take a penalty, and then push the lever to the right, turning to the page labelled **D**
(hint, it's right over there).

SQUEEK & SAUSAGE

The cage slowly descends, creaking. It is closed by a coded lock. Hurry to open it and press the button that will stop the destruction of the planet! No pressure.

It's a button! And not the fun kind of button — the type you'd use on a coat lapel or to make a sock puppet with — but a button that will save the entire world. That's a pretty important button! If only you knew how to get to it.

You think **back** to your briefing but it didn't **cover** this*. Once you have the correct 4-digit code, turn to the pages numbered 101. **You will receive a triple penalty for making an incorrect guess.**

*You can return to the Garden by turning to the pages numbered **51**, the Kitchen on the pages numbered **57**, the Storeroom on the pages numbered **1** and the HQ on the pages labelled **F**.*

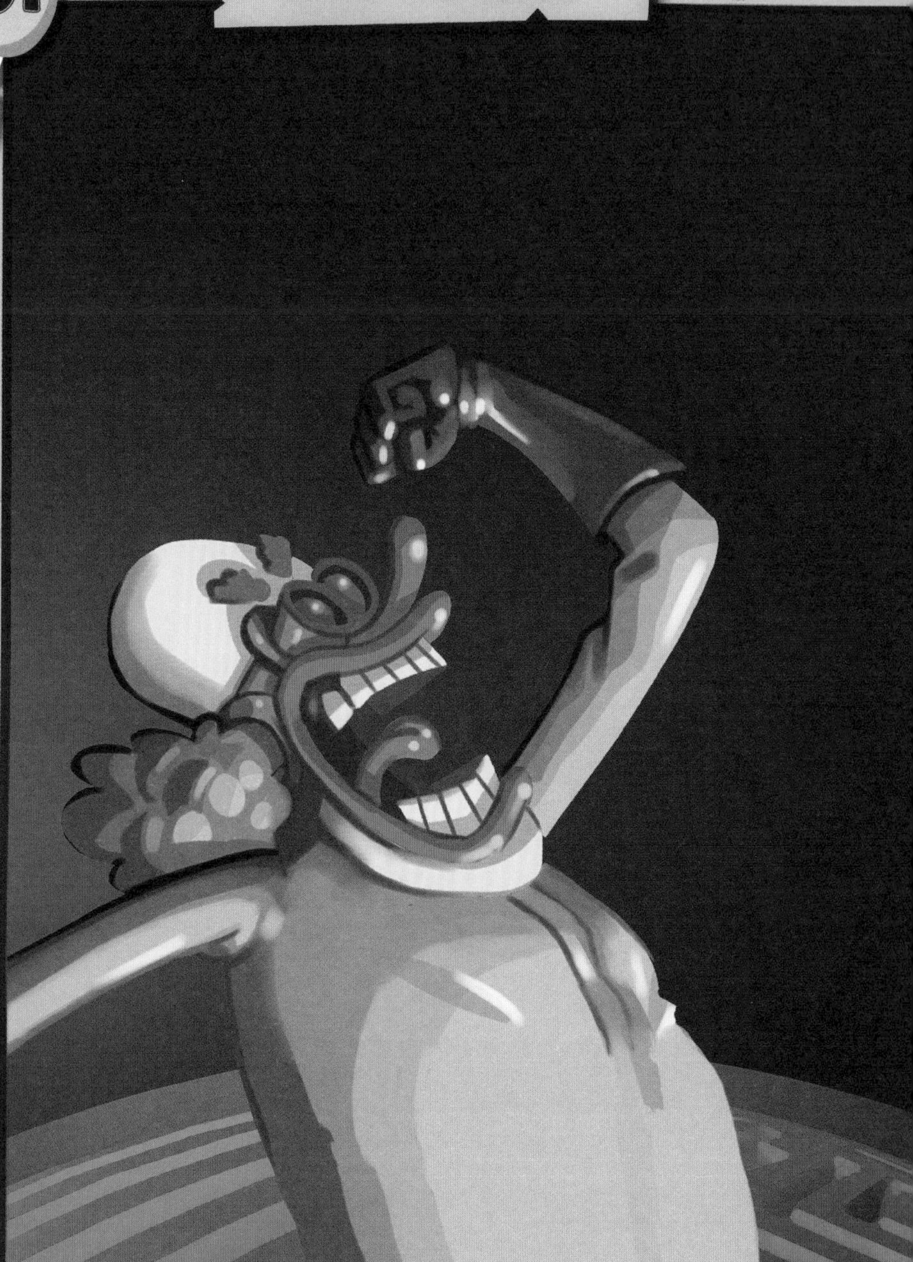

You enter **8792** into the keypad and press the button. Noside's evil device stops after releasing a few electrical flashes. Well done – you have saved the world! That's all, folks!

LOST IN THE TIMEWARP!

Penalties (X):

Notable pages:

Year	Location
'Current' time	Page 0

Red number (object):	Blue number (object):

Codes:

Other notes:

It's the year 2021, and the sky is still rumbling when you arrive at the house of your friend, the eccentric Professor Alcibiades Tempus.

A scientist obsessed with time in all shapes and forms, he asked you to meet him at his home so that you can experiment with his latest invention!

Once there, however, you can't find him anywhere. Neighbours tell you that lightning struck his house. You know the Professor well, and while he is often erratic in his actions, it is unusual for him to completely disappear, or to stand a friend up like this. He must have *hidden* a clue somewhere that will help you find him...

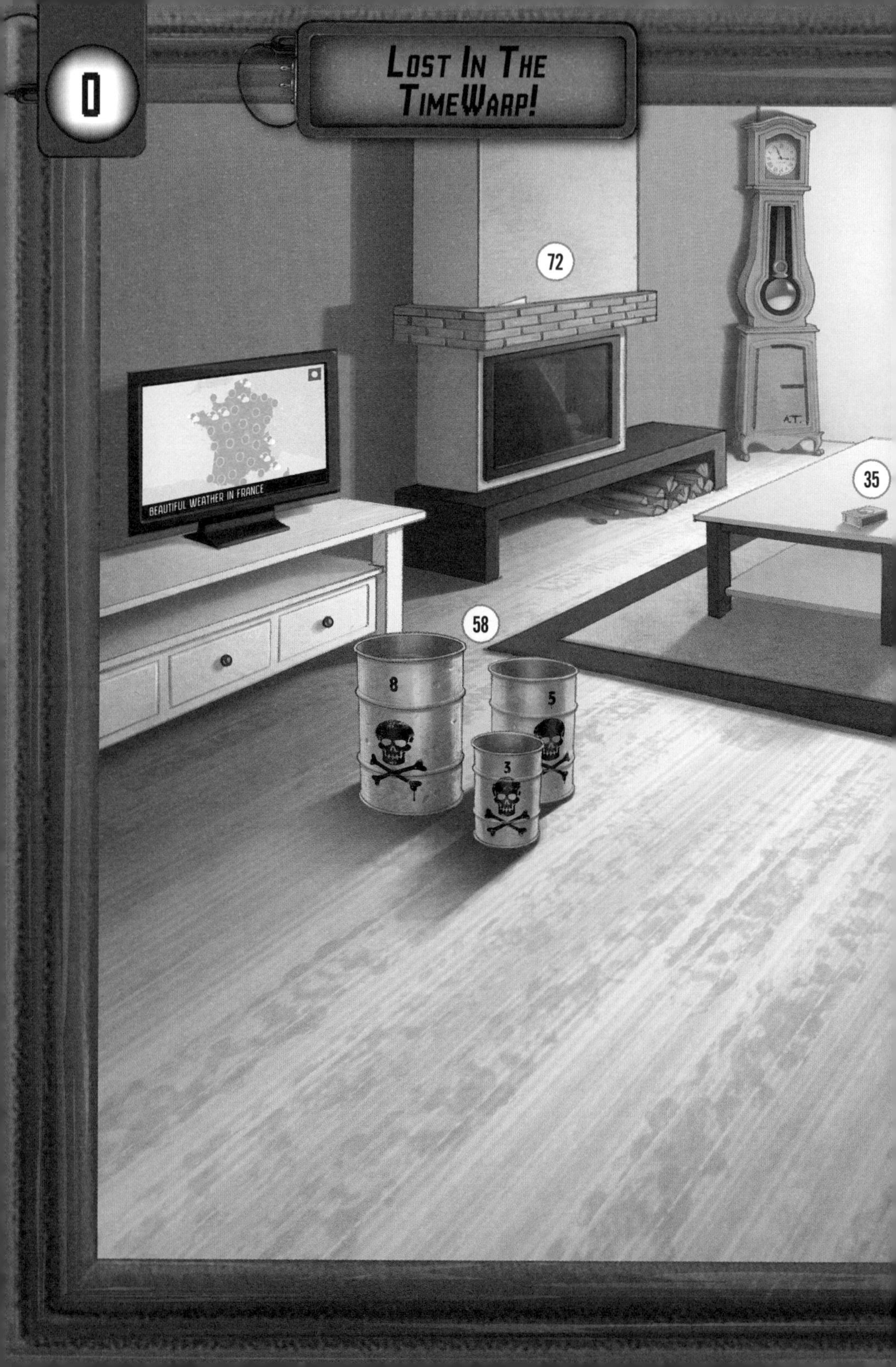
0
Lost In The TimeWarp!
72
35
BEAUTIFUL WEATHER IN FRANCE
A.T.
58
8
5
3

TEMPUS: THE END OF A LINE OF BANKERS?

ALCIBIADES TEMPUS IS A BRILLIANT SCIENTIST, WHOSE FATHER IGOR IS A BRILLIANT BUT RUTHLESS BANKER, AS WERE HIS FOREFATHERS BEFORE HIM. BUT ALCIBIADES HAS DECIDED TO FOLLOW ANOTHER PATH WHICH, ACCORDING TO HIM, WILL DO GREAT FOR HUMANITY. INDEED...

THE DIOSEN CIRCUS IS IN TOWN. CONTINUED ATTRACTIONS.

∞ = infinity

$$(x+a)^n = \sum_{k=0}^{n} \binom{n}{k} x^k a^{n-k}$$

$$= a_o + \sum_{n=1}^{\infty} \left(a_n \cos \frac{n\pi x}{L} + b_n \sin \frac{n\pi x}{L} \right)$$

This unfinished equation, travel to the future will be impossible

As you step into the Professor's living room, you realise that this is the first time you've been alone in his house. Alcibiades is, to the best of your knowledge, the first and only genius you have ever met, and yet his home looks so... ordinary. It still surprises you, every time: a stranger would think that a reasonably successful accountant lived here, not one of science's keenest minds. There are a couple things that stand out to you, however.

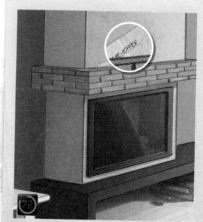

Something strange is stuck IN the mantelshelf! Only a portion of it sticks out from the bricks. You can't retrieve it without damaging it, so you leave it where it is for now.

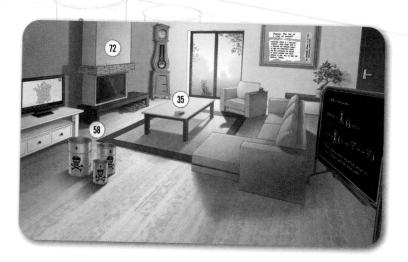

Admittedly, "ordinary" is a relative term. You're so used to the Professor's eccentricities that you barely notice the toxic liquids. It is odd keeping that at home. The first one is filled to the brim, and the others are empty.

This is just a matchbox. Alcibiades doesn't smoke but says he really likes the smell of a newly-struck match.

The house has been in the Tempus family for generations and the Professor clearly feels some deep attachment to it, using it as the base for his experiments rather than setting up a lab of his own. "This is the place to be!" he once exclaimed. "But it's not necessarily the time."

Stop here! To re-examine the living room, return to the pages numbered 0.

You are proud of your tree, but it looks
like it could use a little bit of pruning
maintenance. You take out your trusty
handsaw and get to work.

This is much easier going than
carving a tree, and you soon lose
yourself in the happy rhythm of the
manual labour.

You take care to only remove the dead branches. You feel almost like you are giving a haircut to a beloved child. Was it odd to have formed such a strong bond with a tree so quickly? No odder than time-hopping to stop the apocalypse.

After a lot of effort, you manage to saw off a few of its branches. Stepping back, you are pleased with your efforts. The tree looks much tidier now.

You can return to the Autumn 1974 garden on the pages numbered 6 or the Winter 1950 garden on the pages numbered 77. You can also revisit any of the years listed in your notebook that you have so far discovered.

You return to your own time. The dust raining down from the ceiling tells you it's time to be bold – and maybe find a hazmat suit! Taking a quick decision, you jump back in time to 1900, where...

37

30

...you take an eraser to the house plans and rub the fireplace straight out of history, replacing the plans in the safe. You quickly return to your own time.

The fireplace has vanished! Where it was, a piece of paper lays on its own on the floor.

TIME-HOPPER

M.T.

It looks like a user manual. Admittedly a very crude, hand-drawn one. You don't think this would pass today's health and safety regulations, but they probably don't have them in *Mad Max* times.

Ideally, Martin would have been less ambiguous about what you needed to do, but you've learned that elusiveness runs in the family. Even so, you've got a good idea of what you might need to gather to finally put everything right.

Stop here! You can return to the living room in 1974 by turning to the pages numbered 74 and the autumn 1974 garden on the pages numbered 6, revisit 1950 by turning to the pages numbered 50, return to 1900 on the pages numbered 11 or see a fading image of your current time on the pages numbered 0.

You finish carving S + I into the tree and set a course for 1974, hoping that your declaration of love is enough and that Sophie won't think Igor has just been doing his math homework and etched 5 + 1. If after admiring your handiwork you turned to any page other than here, **take a penalty**.

6 Phew! The Tempus lineage is restored: Igor has started a family. And built a pretty snazzy looking treehouse too. That tree is the gift that keeps on giving.

23

10

10

An old handsaw. It's a little rusty but it still looks handy; you bet it's got a few different uses.

'How come you know my name? Do you know my grandfather?'...

'I just finished my solar energy flashlight.'

"You are _____, aren't you?". He nods. "How come you know my name? Do you know my grandfather?" Although you're currently drawing a blank, you say yes, hoping that the grandfather's identity will somehow come to you as you speak. And it does! "It's _____."

The boy is satisfied by your responses. He seems as relieved as you are. "I just finished my solar energy flashlight," he says, "but now I'm a little bored." Obviously, someone needs an intellectual stimulant.

Another era, another dejected Tempus boy. He's wary about your sudden appearance but is unmistakeably bright - you can tell his brain is whirring away, trying to calculate who you might be. You understand where he's coming from: there are so many members of the Tempus family scattered across the years that it takes you a few moments to work out which one you're talking to. Victor? Alcibiades? Hector? Igor? You also have time to worry you're not starting another nuclear war.

Once you've written down the correct two names that should form your replies in the notebook, you realise that the boy is a BLUE 23 looking for a Red number. You can return to the living room in 1974 by turning to the pages numbered 74, revisit 1950 by turning to the pages numbered 50, revisit 1900 by turning to the pages numbered 11 or see a fading image of your current time on the pages numbered 0.

You enter **40781** and hear an encouraging clinking. The book titles did indeed provide the code that opens the safe: **4** Seasons by Vivaldi, **0** for Oblivion, **7** Deadly Sins, **8** is the Tilted Infinity, and **1** for Solitude. It's a more secure way of hiding than a key under the mat, that's for sure. Perhaps that wasn't a thing yet, back in 1900. If you entered the wrong code, **take a penalty**.

The safe opens! It holds many equities and shares, and a house plan, but that's not why you are here. Although maybe you just leave a note saying INVEST IN GOOGLE… no! Stop messing with the past.

52

This book is in the safe, too. The title is no lie… it's one of the most complex books you have tried to read. It would probably take you several years to understand it!

You wonder, briefly, if you could be convicted of a robbery you've committed a century before your own birth, but if there was ever the case of a crime having extenuating circumstances, the prevention of a nuclear war would surely be it.

Sheet music. This you can understand at least, but you don't recognise any of the songs. They were probably top of the charts back in the day. Apparently the ephemerality of pop music is long-lived.

You should now return to the living room of the year you're currently exploring, which you'll have written in your notebook…

As you place the slippery block next to the fire, you ponder whether this was indeed a less risky approach than using the saw... But the future tech is probably flame resistant. Probably.

22

64

As you wait for it to melt, you ponder all the changes you've made to the world. Who knew that time travel was dangerous? There should definitely be a warning label with the machine. It's irresponsible not to have one, really.

You finally manage to unfreeze an object that seems to have come from the FUTURE! Too bad you don't know how to use it. Or do you?

Someone has carved their initials into the inside of the device. That seems like an expensive bit of defacement of something so valuable, but if today has taught you anything it's that the Tempus family like their initials.

You can revisit any of the years already listed in your notebook, or use this gizmo once you've found instructions on how to do it.

No matter how ornate they are, when they've been in your home long enough you eventually stop noticing decorations. They become a part of the furniture. The furniture does too: in fact, you've rarely paid attention to the longcase clock in this room until just now, when you notice "A.T." scratched into the woodwork, with the number 17 etched into the wood above the letters.

After using a little bit of force to pry it open, the panel of the longcase clock opens and falls at your feet.

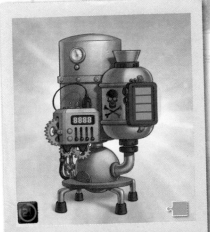

Instinctively, you press one of the buttons on the control panel, but it just sighs robotically. This strange machine seems totally discharged.

DEADLY SINS

GLUTTONY   LUST

GREED   PRIDE   SLOTH

ENVY   WRATH

Published in 1900

You open the book next to the machine. It is brand new but covered in dust. There's a message on an earlier page.

This must be the invention that the Professor wanted your help with. But what sort of machine would you hide inside a clock? And what do the four red bars mean? Maybe it's some kind of elaborate alarm clock. The sort that doesn't let you fall back asleep after you hit its off button in the morning.

To re-examine the living room, return to the pages numbered 0.

An idea strikes you. It seems juvenile, but then so is the broken heart that wrote that diary page. The idea surprised you once by working for a friend back in high school, and love is the universal language. Why shouldn't it work now for Igor?

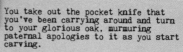

You take out the pocket knife that you've been carrying around and turn to your glorious oak, murmuring paternal apologies to it as you start carving.

It's a good start. Very artistic.
But what could you add inside the
heart to help Igor?

You've never carved a message onto a tree before, and certainly never to reunite a couple who are meant to be together so they can add to their family and avoid the end of days, but you sense that it's probably best to keep things simple: an initial + another initial, maybe even a "4 EVA" if you have the space... no, keep it simple. The letters S, V, H and I spring to mind, but which two could save the world?

Write down the two chosen letters in your notebook. To continue carving, turn to the pages labelled with those letters. You can also return to 1974 by turning to the pages numbered 74, revisit 1950 by turning to the pages numbered 50, revisit 1900 by turning to the pages numbered 11 or see a fading image of your current time on the pages numbered 0.

You feel you are in a maelstrom. It's a sensation beyond anything you've ever experienced, and yet it's also curiously familiar. In a flash of understanding, you realize that you've actually been moving through time for your entire life, but the progress has been so infinitesimal that you haven't been able to perceive it until now. You are thrown into the past. If you wrote any year other than 1900 in your notebook, **take a penalty**.

My friend, you're already here! I just finished hiding the machine and the book in the longcase clock moments ago. What perfect timing.

What a great invention! It will change everything. Let's make the most of the time we have — ha ha! — and see what my house was like in the year 1900. My father Igor often told me about his grandpa Victor. I wonder how he used to live...

Alcibiades is there in the past, waiting for you. He appears remarkably relaxed for someone who has just created the most important invention in the history of... well... time.

Your immediate thought, upon arriving in the distant past, is that it's like one of those museums where you see a room at different points in history. The momentousness of your voyage is somehow less pressing than the change in rug and the slight transit of the clock. For some reason, you thought time travel would be more dramatic than this... with more dinosaurs, for one thing. You turn to Alcibiades to mention this, but he's already darted off into another room.

Write "1900 – Page 11" in your notebook. To continue exploring the 1900 living room, turn to the pages numbered 33.

You patiently explore the living room, chuckling to yourself. Only Alcibiades Tempus would invent a time machine, travel to the dawn of the 20th century and then choose to explore his own house. It's sweet, really. And probably less dangerous than the time-travel movies you've seen. You hope it is, anyway.

An almost full bookcase. It contains so many volumes that even a single gap is conspicuous. Alcibiades' grandfather has probably read every one of these books - what else was there to do back then?

Victor Tempus' safe. Evidently, hiding valuables inside clocks isn't a family tradition.

As he's prone to doing, the Professor is in another room talking to himself. At least, you hope he's talking to himself - surely he wouldn't have invented time travel without at least looking up the grandfather paradox, a consequence which is literally possible given that he's in the home of his actual grandfather.

To enter the garden you see through the window, turn to the pages labelled G.

G

You step into the garden and breathe deeply, letting the past enter your lungs. You're not quite sure what you were expecting - more pollution?

Less pollution? - but everything is roughly the same, at least in this quiet corner of the world.

A pocket knife, good for knifing pockets or wood carving.

82

A butterfly net. You find it
astounding that butterfly collecting
was a genuine hobby once, but it
has always seemed like fun, running
around with a net chasing fluttering
splashes of colour.

14

An old shovel. Assuming that the
Tempus family held onto it, it
would be a really old shovel in
your time.

The shed is so full that it's hard
to remove an object without
everything else clattering about.
Some things never change.

To continue exploring the
garden, turn to the pages
numbered 54.

The idea of time travel is so overwhelming that you can't think about it directly. You focus on the grass under your feet, the pleasantness of the day. This would be a good summer in any year.

54

Such a nice lawn! It's probably kept in good shape for croquet, or whatever people used to play in 1900.

You know something of butterflies, and this one was a rarity, even back in 1900. In fact, it's probably among the last ones of its kind! You can see the street beyond the garden's edge, but it seems rude to explore further without the Professor, as you're essentially his guest in the past. And you're just slightly afraid of messing with time and fraying the edges of the entire universe's existence.

What a beautiful purple lepidopteron! Knowing a word like that, you think Alcibiades isn't the only genius around - with only a hint of smugness.

Stop here! You can return inside the living room by turning to the pages numbered 11. To pop back to the current time, turn to the pages numbered 0, but keep track of where you've been!

It's probably not wise to fool around too much with this garden in the past, but: in for a penny, in for a pound. Speaking of which, if you have a spare few minutes, maybe you should make some wise investments or bet on a sporting event or two.

It is a nice lawn, but when you have a shovel, there's only one thing you can do with it. Dig! You hope there's no angry members of the lawn bowls association around.

That's a lovely looking hole. One of your best. If anything, it's an improvement on the lawn, in your opinion.

Well that was a nice little break in your adventure. There's something very satisfying about hole-digging, no matter what year it is. For a moment you worry about what the Professor will think if he sees it, but that's a problem for some other time.

You can return to any of the living rooms you have so far discovered by turning to the pages you've noted in your notebook.

As you flick through the new-but-dusty book, you spy handwriting that you recognise. You feel a sudden chill: the message would be preposterous coming from anyone else, but you know the Professor… he is telling the truth. He's actually done it, the mad, brilliant fool.

Dear Friends,

This afternoon, an unexpected storm caused a malfunction in the systems of my time machine and I am stuck in the past. Therefore, I hid my machine here. It will wait for you for the years to come. I can't use it without fuel, which only exists in your time. You will need the **exact quantity** to fill it up with.

Join me! I borrowed this book in my day, hoping it won't be missed by anyone.

Your friend,
Professor Alcibiades Tempus

On the first page of the book, a message from Alcibiades Tempus!

Of course the Professor would hide the time machine in a clock. It's so him. You cast your gaze over to the barrels of mysterious fuel that you're about to handle, hoping the liquid isn't corrosive.

It seems you must fuel the machine, but how much exactly do you need?

Write down your movements, transferring fuel from one barrel to another, in the notebook. You must achieve the perfect amount of fuel, and once you have it, you may add 50 Red to a Blue number. You can also re-examine the living room by returning to the pages numbered 0.

How clever of Alcibiades to hide your next year within another timepiece. You enter 1950 into the machine and half a century melts away. It is not dissimilar to the sensation of taking your feet off a treadmill for a few moments while the belt continues going around and around. The landing is just as tricky to stick, too. 1950, here we come! If you entered the wrong year into your notebook, **take a penalty**.

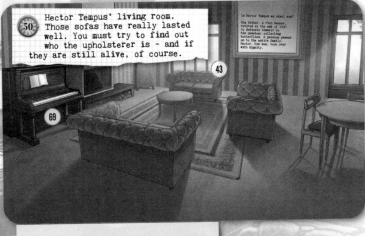

50 — Hector Tempus' living room. Those sofas have really lasted well. You must try to find out who the upholsterer is - and if they are still alive, of course.

43

69

69

The piano of the Professor's forefather. You release the metronome and play a few bars that are stuck in your head, absent-mindedly.

One tune matches the timing exactly, with the eight notes ringing out across the living room while the metronome ticks along, perfectly corresponding to the first, third, fifth and seventh notes.

The garden looks somewhat less inviting in 1950. Perhaps you should pop back to modern day and get a nice warm winter coat?

You courageously brave the cold, snow crunching under your feet, and explore the garden. It's winter now, so if you were more pedantic you'd say that technically you've travelled 50 years and a few months.

Stop here! Write down "1950 – page 50" in your notebook. You can return to 1900 by turning to the pages numbered 11 or see a fading image of your current time on the pages numbered 0. If you'd like to use the time machine to travel to a new time, turn to the page of the last two numbers in the year you want to travel to.

It takes some heaving, but you manage to tip the fuel from barrel to barrel until you end up with the perfect amount of fuel: four units, enough to turn each of the red bars to green. If you did not end up with four units of fuel, **take a penalty**.

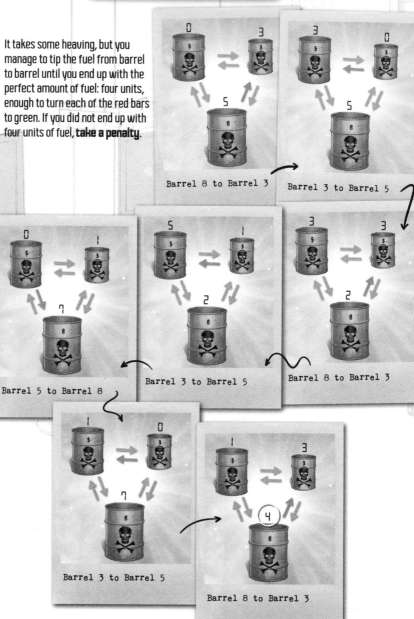

Barrel 8 to Barrel 3

Barrel 3 to Barrel 5

Barrel 5 to Barrel 8

Barrel 3 to Barrel 5

Barrel 8 to Barrel 3

Barrel 3 to Barrel 5

Barrel 8 to Barrel 3

The time machine is operational. It
is now possible to do a few trips
into the past! You weren't expecting
this when you turned up - just a cup
of tea and a biscuit.

Perhaps you're just woozy from the fumes, but
you're very impressed with yourself for filling
the machine so precisely without getting any
fuel on your skin. In retrospect, gloves would
have been a sensible option, especially given
the skull and crossbones on the fuel tank.

To use the time machine, enter the correct year in your notebook and
turn to the pages numbered 11. You can also look again at the living room
on the pages numbered 0 or the longcase clock on the pages numbered 17.

Hopefully this vicarious declaration of love will be enough to sway Sophie, although the S doesn't quite look exactly like an S... It has hints of some other symbol. Perhaps you need to work on your woodworking.

You can return to the uncarved heart on the pages numbered 45 or turn to another letter. Once you've completed your message, add it together and what do you get?

V! Leave Victor out of it.
That would be weird.

Take a penalty and return to the pages numbered 45.

As you put the book back on the shelf, you feel a tiny change wash over you, as if the universe has shifted slightly in its seat. You can't figure out what exactly is different, so you decide to head back to the modern day to make sure nothing dramatic has happened.

Phew… the only difference you can see is that the article pinned to the wall has changed. No big deal.

That quote from Victor Tempus is rather cryptic, and you wonder if he would still feel that way if he knew about Netflix. On balance, you think so, and anyway it gives you a very bookish idea. You hurry back to 1900.

Victor Tempus' safe is beguiling. Can you crack the code?

You may now be able to open the safe. Once you have the five-digit code, turn to page Y. You can also revisit the current living room by turning to the pages numbered 0.

Initially there doesn't seem to be much
of interest for you in the garden, or at
least anything interesting is buried
under three feet of snow. In your
summer clothes, you feel as if you
are justified in your assumption that
anything worth finding will be back in
the warmth of the house. But then...

43 On closer inspection, however,
there's something suspended in
the pond. You sigh, and go to
investigate.

12

The basin is entirely frozen. You notice a weird gizmo stuck in the ice - you are pretty sure from your time with the Professor that gizmo is the technical term.

You only manage to scrape the surface while trying to extract it. Without winter wear or tools, this is a fool's errand, and you like to think that you are no fool. Then you remember that you caught a butterfly in 1900 and caused a nuclear war, and decide you might need to revise your assumptions about yourself.

Return to the living room in 1950 by turning to the pages numbered 50. You can also return to 1900 by turning to the pages numbered 11 or see a fading image of your current time on the pages numbered 0.

Young Alcibiades grins at the sight of the book; perhaps he's the only person in history who could be actively excited by Diophantine equations. This warm glow must be what it feels like to be a teacher.

The youngster runs inside the house, in his excitement already forgetting the fact that you just appeared out of nowhere right in front of him.

As you leave the past he's already too absorbed in reading to say goodbye. You hope he will have digested the book's contents in the intervening years, but upon arriving back in your own time, you flick on the TV and you're disappointed to find that you still haven't undone the apocalypse. This really isn't turning into a very good day. Something has changed, though...

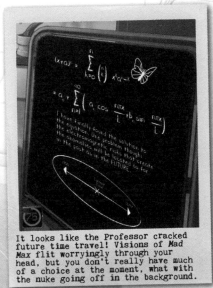

It looks like the Professor cracked future time travel! Visions of Mad Max flit worryingly through your head, but you don't really have much of a choice at the moment, what with the nuke going off in the background.

If you didn't add "Alcibiades" and then "Hector" to your notebook, *take a penalty*. The blackboard should give you the information needed to make another trip in time. When you've figured it out, write down the destination year in your notebook and travel to the pages numbered 83. You can also return to the living room in 1974 by turning to the pages numbered 74, revisit 1950 by turning to the pages numbered 50, revisit 1900 by turning to the pages numbered 11 or see a fading image of your current time on the pages numbered 0.

Throwing all caution to the wind, you plant the acorn in 1900 inside your freshly dug hole. You knew there was a reason for all that digging.

68

9

+

77 — Gardening complete, you return to the winter of 1950. You're thankful to have not caused an even-earlier calamity than your previous little mistake, and instead gaze proudly upon the relatively young oak tree you have just called into existence.

28

19

A 50-year-old (or minus-24-year-old, depending on how you think about it) oak tree with a thick trunk and a few bare branches.

Delighted by the tree's growth, you impetuously yell, "Look on my Works, ye Mighty, and despair!", and fortunately there's no-one around to hear you. It felt good. You have no regrets.

You can return to 1974 by turning to the pages numbered 74, revisit 1950 by turning to the pages numbered 50, revisit 1900 by turning to the pages numbered 11 or see a fading image of your current time on the pages numbered 0.

The well is still frozen, but you notice something else worthy of your attention. You try to ignore it, because spending more time in this icy patch is not top of your list of priorities, even if you have just created life in it. But five more minutes in the cold is probably worth it to stop a nuclear explosion and bring your friend back to life... just.

You clamber up the tree. Hidden in a wooden box, you find the diary Igor used to keep when he was a child.

> I don't like this tree. When I am all growned-up, I will cut it down. I don't like butterflies either. They should all be kept in a display case. We all do that in the family. I love Sophie, but she loves nature and butterflies! She doesn't want to marry me anymore because I told her I want to catch them. If only I could tell her that I love her... But without help, I will never dare.

That poor boy. He's practically Romeo. You need to find some way to get his life back on track. And hopefully not end up like it did for Romeo.

Even at a young age, Igor has a habit of going to high places when he's upset. You feel guilty reading through his diary but all of reality is at stake, which seems more important at the moment than his privacy.

You can return to the garden in the winter of 1950 by turning to the pages numbered 77. You can also return to 1974 by turning to the pages numbered 74, revisit 1950 by turning to the pages numbered 50, revisit 1900 by turning to the pages numbered 11 or see a fading image of your current time on the pages numbered 0.

Oops... It seems that catching the butterfly with the net in the past has triggered something awful to happen! Professor Tempus, waving at you from inside the house, disappears right before your eyes as if he was never born. You rush back to the time machine to travel back to the current time.

It's the butterfly effect for sure. It seems you've inadvertently caused a nuclear war. Ashton Kutcher was right.

Preserved butterflies in a display case. They look pretty, sure, but was it worth it??

Four connected hourglasses. Impulsively, you turn them over and watch the sand slide away.

What a pity that you happened to erase the Professor from history: he would absolutely know what to do about you erasing him from history. It's undeniable that you need to undo the damage somehow, but you're not sure that the answer lies in 1900.

You can revisit the house in 1900 by turning to the pages numbered 11, or see a fading image of the present day by turning to the pages numbered 0. To use the time machine to travel to a new year, head to the last two digits of the year that is your destination, but you may want to do some... tidying first, if you haven't already.

You sit on the lip of the pond basin and decide that it is time to extract the gizmo using the handsaw. You really wish you had gloves.

It takes absolutely ages - this is not what the saw is designed for. Nevertheless, the trusty saw does its job. You have what you came for!

22

A block of ice with a weird gizmo inside. Although you can't fully see it within the fogged ice, it's plain that the technology doesn't belong to 1950, or even later in the 20th century.

The block of ice slides right out, but you decide not to cut any deeper in case you damage the device. You'll need to find another way to get rid of the remaining ice.

You can return to the Autumn 1974 garden on the pages numbered 6 or the Winter 1950 garden on the pages numbered 77. You can also revisit any of the years listed in your notebook.

Time waits for no-one: there was obviously some important reason to visit 1950 other than catching a chill, but no sooner have you arrived than you're leaving again. Following the musical clues in the "Quartet for the end of times", you head to 1974. Groovy. If you entered any other date into the time travel machine, **take a penalty**.

Wow, a pinball machine! This has to be your favourite time period yet. You pat your pockets for loose change, but you're out of luck. Better get exploring instead.

You find a few pencils and an eraser on the table. Maybe if you maim a few more butterflies with some flying pencils you can undo this whole mess.

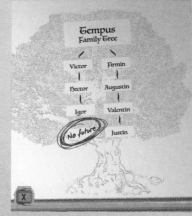

Tempus
Family Tree

Victor   Firmin

Hector   Augustin

Igor   Valentin

No future Justin

Alcibiades' name no longer appears on this document. It's as if his existence has been entirely erased from this reality, which, thanks to you, it has.

The lights of the pinball machine blink on and off. As you contemplate the living room's décor, one fact is clearly evident: this is the home of a single person.

Write down "1974 – page 74" in your notebook. To go into the garden, turn to the pages numbered 46.

You head out into the autumnal garden, and you are surprised to hear a scrabbling coming from above your head. Looking up, you spot a morose and unkempt man on the roof!

He starts shouting at you while gesticulating wildly. You would be staying more still if you were way up there, but you get the feeling this is not his first trip onto the roof.

Something is not right. Igor Tempus, who should have been Alcibiades' father, looks and sounds like he is leading the life of a bitter loner, albeit one who has become excellent at pinball. And now he's taken refuge on the roof where it is impossible to reach him without his ladder.

Gleaning an acorn in autumn...
What could be more normal? It's nice
to hold onto some sense of normality
at the moment, what with all this
time travel and apocalypse going on
around you.

When he first scurried onto the roof and pulled the ladder up after him, you assumed that Igor was distressed by you materialising in his home. That's a pretty natural reaction, thinking about it. But all your attempts to coax him down are met with grouchy grumbling. He's clearly so wary of strangers that he would have reacted that way even if you'd shown up at the front door.

Stop here! You can re-examine the living room in 1974 by turning to the pages numbered 74, revisit 1950 by turning to the pages numbered 50, revisit 1900 by turning to the pages numbered 11 or see a fading image of your current time on the pages numbered 0. Time travel is *exhausting*.

The freezing cold gives you an idea, one which should add both to your comfort and to your quest to save the world! It's a win-win.

It's time to start a fire, and not the apocalyptic kind either. Just a nice, small, warming one in the garden. The smell of the wood smoke is very comforting.

This roaring bonfire is impressive
- you're a proper survivalist at
heart. That might come in handy if
you have to go back to the future.

You're so glad that you held onto those
matches from your first visit to the Tempus
home. You feel the heat on your face as the
wood pops and sizzles. You think that it would
melt pretty much anything.

You can return to the Autumn 1974 garden on the pages numbered 6 or the
Winter 1950 garden on the pages numbered 77. You can also revisit any of
the years already listed in your notebook.

"The anomalies will be located as far in the past as in the future", the Professor wrote, so your destination was the same number of years into the future as the years between 1900 and your current time. For a moment you struggle to remember the "real year" - your time travel has taken its toll - but then you remember it is 2021. You therefore travel to the year 2142. If you wrote down the wrong year in your notebook, **take a penalty**.

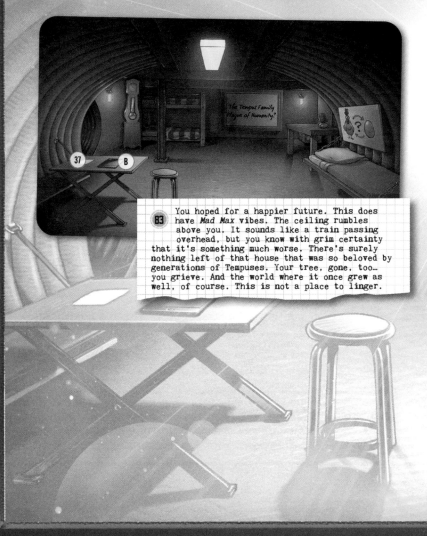

83 You hoped for a happier future. This does have *Mad Max* vibes. The ceiling rumbles above you. It sounds like a train passing overhead, but you know with grim certainty that it's something much worse. There's surely nothing left of that house that was so beloved by generations of Tempuses. Your tree, gone, too… you grieve. And the world where it once grew as well, of course. This is not a place to linger.

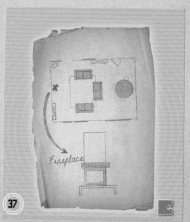

37

Among the many documents that have been saved, you find plans of the house dating back to 1900. This is when Victor Tempus had a fireplace built. All gone now...

83 On the tablet's screen is a blog post, apparently written by a future Tempus descendant.

Martin Tempus' Time Travel Blog

1 : An incident deriving from a butterfly in 1900 seems to be the cause of the nuclear holocaust. Based on my calculations, I am still in a temporal pocket that will allow me to correct this.

2 : I have sent objects to the past to help. This limits the risks of a time paradox.

3 : I have also sent the time-hopper and its user manual which should help in resolving the cause of all of this. I intend to rectify the time curve and restore my family's reputation.

Stop here! You can return to the living room in 1974 by turning to the pages numbered 74 and the autumn 1974 garden on the pages numbered 6, revisit 1950 by turning to the pages numbered 50, return to 1900 on the pages numbered 11 or see a fading image of your current time on the pages numbered 0.

LOST IN THE TIMEWARP!

H! Hector is a lovely fellow, I'm sure, but there's no need to state it by carving it on the tree.

Take a penalty and return to the pages numbered 45.

Adding that I for Igor was simple, both
because you've already met him and
because it's just a straight line.

You can return to the uncarved heart on the pages numbered 45 or turn to
another letter. Once you've completed your message, add it together and
what do you get?

You pull out the highly detailed user manual sent to you from the future and analyze its contents. It seems to be indicating that you need to subtract something from the gizmo in order to undo your time-travelling woes. If you used the gizmo incorrectly, **take a penalty**.

-86-

- NOT +

The butterfly was what started this whole mess - that moment of beautiful madness when you caught it in the net. It's time to fix things.

BEAUTIFUL WEATHER IN FRANCE

A flash! You look around you in 1950 and you feel a subtle shift, a universal sigh, almost as if all of reality was relaxing. Is that possible? You shrug. Who is to say what it and isn't possible when the Tempus family are around.

You've done so much traipsing through time that you only have enough fuel left for one last trip. The time has come to return to your starting point and meet with the professor. You've saved the Earth! Nobody will ever know, but given that you're the one caused the problems in the first place, maybe that's for the best...

Note the year of your final destination in your notebook and travel to the pages numbered 99.

The machine starts smoking. You are back to the current time, but it is impossible to travel any further without fuel or a fix to the machine.

You should have written 2021 in your notebook - if you haven't, **take a penalty**.

You made it my friend! The world is saved! As am I – it felt quite odd not to exist for a while, I have to admit. Now, listen carefully. You must destroy this machine!

"It is too dangerous. You must complete this task because it was you that brought about the **butterfly** effect in the **current time period**."

"To deactivate the machine permanently, you'll have to press four buttons in the correct order. You will receive a **triple penalty** for making an incorrect guess. Good luck!"

Time is against you, but when isn't it? The only clue you have to solving this puzzle is the emphasis the Professor put on certain words. The contraption shudders like a washing machine. Any moment now, it will surely tear an irrevocable hole in the temporal fabric of the universe. You can barely understand that sentence, let alone what the consequences will be.

Once you have the final code, write it down in your notebook and turn to the pages numbered 100.

LOST IN THE TIMEWARP!

You press green - green - purple - blue on the keypad. The room shakes, the machine crackles and disappears before your eyes in a blinding flash. It's probably for the best, and the butterflies fluttering outside will not say otherwise.

Playing with the threads of time is just as thrilling as it is dangerous, but a too-great power entails a too-great responsibility! You look over at Alcibiades, but he has already turned to his blackboard where he is busying himself with his next great invention - as if you hadn't just averted a nuclear apocalypse, or he hadn't been briefly winked out of existence.

Quietly, you let yourself out of the house and decide that it is time for a nice long nap.

Solutions

The Reception Room

In the reception room, first take the coat key [33 Blue] that is hidden in the lab coat's pocket [42 Blue].

To find the second key, pour the water from the well-watered vase [57 Blue] into the hole in the box [27 Red]. ([27 Red] + [57 Blue] = 84.) Take the vase key [84 Blue].

Use the vase key [84 Blue] to open the door of the generator room [8 Red]. ([8 Red] + [84 Blue] = 92.)

The Generator Room

In the Generator Room [92 Grey] the number 7 is hiding on the upper right side of the generator. Go to 7 to find the glass slide [7 Blue]. Examine it under the microscope ([66 Red] + [7 Blue] = 73) and you turn to 73 to get a clue to a further puzzle.

As for the slide [13 Blue], just insert it into the projector in the reception room ([13 Blue] + [12 Red] = 25) to reveal a hidden door. You cannot open it yet, unfortunately.

The coat key [33 Blue] opens the filing cabinet ([33 Blue] + [47 Red] = 80). You find the UV lamp [80 Blue].

The lamp [80 Blue] is then used to light the generator's keypad ([80 Blue] + [11 Red] = 91). This shows you which keys have fingerprints. The sign ">" means "greater than" and indicates that you must enter the numbers in a descending order: **8652**. Turn to K. You can now add a 15 [Blue jigsaw with the number 15] to a red number, representing it receiving electrical power.

The flexible copper wire [50 Blue] found in the reception room is to be placed on the electric panel [F Green] using clue 73 from the glass slide [50 Blue] + 73 = 123). The clue – 4-3-4 in red, green and yellow – shows you where the wire must be fixed: the 4th pin of the 1st and 3rd rows, and the 3rd pin of the 2nd row. 1 + 7 + 1 = 9 [9 Red]. Thus [9 Red] + [50 Blue] = 59. Turn to page 59 and you find the phone has started ringing: 27 [27 Blue].

The Generator Room cont.

Combine the ringing phone sound [27 Blue] with the wall-mounted phone ([27 Blue] + [37 Red] = 64) to get the working phone [64 Yellow].

The working phone [64 Yellow] is to be combined with the wing drawn on a piece of paper [L Grey]. The letters **W, I, N, G** when matched against the dial form the code **9464**. Provided you have activated the generator, you can turn to page R.

Once on page R, follow the instructions in the professor's letter Y to learn how to activate the control panel B:

The switch on the right: +2
Press the black button 4 times: +4
Press the red button 10 times: +10

This gives a total of 16 [16 Red], to be added to the working generator's energy ([16 Red + [15 Blue] = 31). Turn to 31 and you hear a click nearby, which is the sound of the hidden door opening. This now allows you to go through to the laboratory on page 56. ([25 Red] + [31 Blue] = 56).

The Formula Final Score:

0 penalties:	Amazing job!
1-2 penalties:	Great job!
3-5 penalties:	Okay job!
6-8 penalties:	Was this your first job?
9+ penalties:	Please don't make this your day job.

The Laboratory

In the laboratory, the reinforced chest [28 Red] can be opened by noting the Mona Lisa picture and reading the Periodic Table of elements [3 Red]. Mo:5 Na:3 Li:2 Sa:7 means **5327** is the correct code. Turn to page M and inside the chest W you find the LP record [23 Blue] and more coloured vials [93 Blue].

Place the LP record [23 Blue] on the record player [20 Red]. ([23 Blue] + [20 Red] = 43). Turn to page 43.

The turntable is playing backwards, so you reverse the code: 1234 becomes **4321**

Turn to page H. The message tells you to add 11 to the safe [74], so 11 + 74 = 85. Turn to page 85.

The letters of the files refer to the planets on the poster [2 Red], e.g. the first letters of **U**ranus, **V**enus, **S**aturn, etc. Only the "**N**" for **N**eptune is missing, corresponding to the question mark. Turn to page N.

The Formula reveals 4 numbers, coloured in blue, red, green and grey.

Now, count the number of identically-coloured vials [93 Blue] in the opened armored safe W and the medicine cabinet [90 Red]. 1 grey, 2 blue, 3 red, 4 green. That's the order that the numbers from the Formula should be entered into the keypad: **8563**. Turn to Page C to enter them into the keypad and you escape through the exit.

Well done! Now, how many penalties did you get along the way?

SQUEEK & SAUSAGE

The Storeroom

First, find the light switch to turn on the lights. Turn to page [J Grey]. The light needs to be turned into the "on position", from the "off position". Get it? You do that by going to page [1 Grey].

If you look closely on the right corner of the VCR [91 Red] a VHS cassette is hidden [18 Blue].

The instruction on the cassette reads "Rewind" backwards. So look at its number upside down, changing 18 into 81! Turn to page [81 Blue].

Put the VHS cassette in the TV/VCR combo: [81 Blue]+[11 Red]= [92 Grey]. Turn to page [92 Grey].

Noside's laugh hEhE, when read upside down, gives you the code to door [P Yellow]: **3434**. Turn to page F to enter it. Now you're in…

The HQ

Underneath the mat marked 46 is key [46 Blue] which you find by turning to page [46 Blue].

Combine the glass of water [24 Blue] with the fridge [H Grey], making a skull shaped ice-cube [Red jigsaw with the number 30]+[24 Blue] = [54 Blue]

Then use the cube to open the door with the skull slot: [54 Blue]+[3 Red] = [57 Grey]. Turn to page [57 Grey].

The Kitchen

A mouse is hiding in his hole: Turn to page [20 Grey] to meet him.

The poster [41 Red] has **6** orange squid arms, **7** purple and **5** green. The lock on the desk requires a code related to these colours: **7656** (purple, orange, green, orange). Turn to page [9 Grey] to enter the code and find the sleeping pill [6 Blue]. The drawer [9 Grey] also has 3 hidden numbers: the recipe [78 Grey], the instructions [4 Grey] and the music score [37 Grey]. Visit those pages to see the relevant information.

To find the code of the cupboard's combination lock [63 Yellow], look at the recipe [78 Grey]. The cheddar must be added half an hour (30 mins) after the baking has started, so add 30 mins to the start time displayed on the oven [89 Red]: 1217+30= **1247.** Turn to page [32 Grey] to get the cheese [32 Blue].

The Kitchen cont.

Use the piece of cheese to lure the mouse: [32 Blue]+ [20 Red]= [52 Grey]. Turn to page [52 Grey] and receive the captured mouse [52 Blue].

Now you have all the maze pieces you assemble them and turn to page [100 Grey].

Now looking at the completed maze you must decide which hole to put the mouse [52 Blue] in. 25 is the correct path to the sausage so [Red jigsaw with the number 25]+[52 Blue]= [77 Grey]. Go to page [77 Grey] to receive the titular sausage [77 Red].

Stick the sleeping pill in the sausage: [6 Blue]+[77 Red]= [83 Grey]. Go to page [83 Grey] to get the sleepy sausage [83 Blue].

Now throw this at the watchdog behind the door [7 Red]: [7 Red]+[83 Blue]= [90 Grey]. Turn to page [90 Grey].

Noside remotely locks the door [5 Red] but luckily you still have the key [46 Blue]. [46 Blue]+ [5 Red]= [51 Grey]. Turn to page [51 Grey].

Squeek & Sausage Final Score:

0 penalties:	Brilliant work!
1-2 penalties:	Terrific work!
3-5 penalties:	Acceptable work!
6-8 penalties:	Just made it work!
9+ penalties:	Security has been called to escort you from the premises.

The Little Garden

Plant the little seeds: [14 Blue]+ [58 Red]=[72 Grey]. Turn to page [72 Grey].

But for the seeds to grow they need to be watered. Assembling the pipes correctly gives you 2+6+5+3= [Red jigsaw with the number 16].

[72 Blue]+[Red jigsaw with the number 16]= [88 Grey]. Turn to page [88 Grey] to see the unusual flowers.

The flowers match up to the music score [37 Grey], with the fence as the stave. The blue flower symbol on the padlock [R Yellow] gives a clue that it's the blue flowers positions that is important: **3154**. Turn to page [36 Grey] to enter the code.

The Final Puzzle

Inspect the mechanism [36 Grey] carefully to note how all the wheels and gears turn when the lever is pulled. To get the arrow to point at the down icon you must pull the lever to the right: Turn to page [D Grey].

To deactivate the lasers, follow the clues to go to the BACK COVER of this book! The numbers you need are in the ISBN Number above the bar code, indicated by 4 stars: **8792**!

You did it!

Hopefully not just by reading this entire solution. I'm sure you didn't… Did you?

Living Room – Alcibiades Tempus – 2021

First note that the number 17 is hidden on the front of the long-case clock. Turn to page 17.

The Book [79 Blue] has a number in the corner indicating a message from the Professor. Turn to page 1.

The message from Alcibiades Tempus tells you that you need the correct fuel quantity for the machine to work. According to the red lights, four parts of fuel are needed.

To get four parts of fuel in one barrel you should move the fuel in this order:
Barrel 8 to barrel 3 - barrel 3 to barrel 5 - barrel 8 to barrel 3 - barrel 3 to barrel 5 - barrel 5 to barrel 8 - barrel 3 to barrel 5 - barrel 8 to barrel 3.

Fill the machine with the four parts of fuel: 50+ [21 Blue]= 71.

The only available year you know is 1900, located at the bottom of the page in book [79 Blue]. Enter that in your notebook.

Living Room And Garden – Victor Tempus – 1900

The butterfly is so beautiful, you can't resist catching it with your net: [13 Red]+ [82 Blue] = 95. Oops, you caused WW3. That's the butterfly effect for you! Put the book [79 Blue] back in the bookcase:
[79 Blue]+[18 Red]= 97.

The quote in the article hints that the spines in the books hold the key to the safe's code.

Look at the titles, they all have a number:
- Vivaldi's **4** seasons
- Oblivion equals **0**
- The **7** deadly sins (after putting the book back)
- The Tilted Infinity equals **8** (because the infinity symbol is a tilted 8)
- Solitude is **1**

The code is **40781**.

Living Room – Alcibiades Tempus – 2021

Once you have done that you need to find the next year to visit. The clue lies in the hourglasses [55 Green]. In the second image you can see sand has flowed through them at different speeds and they have numbers on their bases.

The year to visit is indicated by the hourglasses' numbers from fastest to slowest: **1**, **9**, **5** and **0**. Turn to page 50.